RICHARD BRAKE was born in 19
were of the Second World War, a
English and German fighter plane

CW00820751

He was educated at Bristol Gr
enjoyed the sporting activities but, nonetheless, still managed to pass
his exams. During his first job with a builders merchant he was called
up for National Service with the Royal Air Force. Most of the time
was spent near Tripoli in Libya, and on one occasion he was called out
to help fight locusts, which were threatening all the crops on the edge
of the Sahara Desert. During this time he again enjoyed sport, and
after this period of service continued to pursue his interest in football,
rugby and squash. Following retirement he turned to bowls.

Most of Richard's career was spent in a commercial finance
environment and involved negotiations with clients in a wide variety
of industries.

He was a founder member of a local Round Table in his thirties
and former member of 41 Club.

He married Joan in 1958 and had three sons. Their lives were
turned upside down, however, when in his mid-forties their eldest son
died at the age of 21. This led to a spiritual search for the meaning of
life and a subsequent quest for ancient teachings and wisdom. They
visited India several times and spent two months in the USA at an
Academy for the study of A Course in Miracles.

With the passing of his wife in 2012 Richard gradually developed
a gift of channelling which has resulted in this unique and inspirational
book *Light the Way*.

If you'd like to send Richard an email you can contact him at
lightthewaybook@btinternet.com.

Light the Way

A Collection of Inspired Spiritual Teachings by Joyful One

Richard Brake

To June
With love and blessings
Richard
+ +

SilverWood

Published in 2014 by SilverWood Books

SilverWood Books Ltd
30 Queen Charlotte Street, Bristol, BS1 4HJ
www.silverwoodbooks.co.uk

Copyright © Richard Brake 2014

The right of Richard Brake to be identified as the author
of this work has been asserted by him in accordance with the
Copyright, Designs and Patents Act 1988.

All rights reserved. No part of this publication may be reproduced,
stored in a retrieval system, or transmitted in any form or by any means,
electronic, mechanical, photocopying, recording or otherwise,
without prior permission of the copyright holder.

The text in this book is written as it was received during channelling
sessions. Errors in grammar and punctuation may be present, as all attempts
have been made to preserve the original voice.

ISBN 978-1-78132-279-6 (paperback)
ISBN 978-1-78132-280-2 (ebook)

British Library Cataloguing in Publication Data
A CIP catalogue record for this book is available from
the British Library

Set in Bembo by SilverWood Books
Printed on responsibly sourced paper

*This book is dedicated to Joan Brake, my wife,
soul mate and best friend, who shared my life on earth
and is still with me from the world of spirit.*

Contents

Acknowledgements	*11*
Foreword	*12*
Preface	*14*
Introduction	*15*

Part One

How the Book Came to be Written	*19*

Part Two

Universal Love	*25*
The Now	*27*
Inspiration	*28*
Slide	*29*
Think of Me	*30*

Part Three

The Human Race	*33*
Nature	*35*
The Search	*37*
Peace	*39*
Light	*40*
Time	*42*
The Silence	*44*
Living in the Now	*46*
New Day	*48*
The Life Force	*50*
New Year Opportunity	*51*
New Age Vibrations	*53*
I AM That	*55*
All's Well that Ends Well	*56*
Energy	*58*
Essence of Life	*59*
Channelling	*60*

Knowledge	62
Golden Refuge	64
Point of No Return	66
Golden Ray	68
Judgements	70
I in You and You in Me	72
Happiness	74
Endurance	76
Changing Vibrations	78
Crossroads	80
Universal Power	82
Cause and Effect	84
Closeness to God	86
The Book of Life	87
Moribund or Carefree	90
More to Life and Death	93

Part Four

Infinite Life	97
Foundations	98
Heaven or Hell	100
A Hint of Spirit Life	102
Relationships	104
Angelic Forces	106
At the Start of the Day	108
All That Is	110
Moment to Moment	112
Life on Earth	114
Diversity to Unity	116
Everlasting Moment	118
The Sound of Silence	120
At the Ready	122
Re-Awakening	124
Stepping-Stones	126
The Truth Within	128
Live in Love and Peace	130
The Narrow or Wide Road	132

Microscopic World	134
The Storehouse Within	136
I AM	138
I AM Everywhere	139
I AM One with All	140

Part Five

The Living Planet	145
Unseen Colours	146
Friend	147
The Continuity of Life	148
Gamesmanship	150
Conditions on Earth	152
Your World	154
Love	155
Embrace all Life	157
New Relationships	158
The Purpose of Life	160
Live by the Teachings	162
How is your Boat?	164
Pause for a Moment	165
Face to Face with the Lord	166
The Moment	168
Journey Within	169
Inner Light	170
One-Pointedness	171
Communion with Spirit Within	172
At One with All That Is	174
Conscious, Conscience, Consciousness	175
Enlightenment	176
I AM in You and You are in Me	177

Part Six

Welcome	181
Change	182
In the Now	184
Peace Within	185
Sunrise	186

Meditation	*187*
Silence in the Moment	*188*
Meditation in Love and Service	*189*
Holy Grail	*190*
New Dawn	*191*
Primordial Love	*192*
The New Heaven on Earth	*193*
Epilogue	*194*
Appendices	
Appendix A Personal Letters	*196*
Appendix B Circle Meetings	*204*
Appendix C Personal Teachings	*210*
Appendix D Quotations	*216*

Acknowledgements

I am not a writer and it seems natural, therefore, to acknowledge with love and gratitude the real authors of this book, known as Joyful One, who are a group of teachers from the next world.

Many friends and family encouraged me to collate the channelled articles into a book and I am, indeed, grateful to them all. One family member, Jane Ducker, kindly donated a photograph and idea for the front cover, for which I am so appreciative.

Special mention must be given to Janet and Brian Passmore, Janet for the editing and proofreading and to both of them for their patience in listening to the work, especially in the early days, and for their undoubted love, confidence, advice and dedication to the project.

Equally I would like to thank Aimé and Sandra Levy, Aimé for the hours he has spent converting the contents into a readily presentable manuscript, and I am indebted to Sandra for writing the foreword. Both have given their love and utmost support for this special assignment.

I acknowledge with thanks permission from Findhorn Press to use quotations from *Opening Doors Within* © Eileen Caddy 1986. Edited and compiled by David Earl Platts. Published by Findhorn Press, Scotland. Entries for 25 March, 29 May, 17 and 19 July.

I also acknowledge a quotation from *The Aquarian Gospel of Jesus the Christ* by Levi, which is now in the public domain, and short quotations from Rabindranath Tagore (1861 – 1941) and R W Emerson (1803 – 1882).

Foreword

It is an honour for me to write the foreword to this extraordinary book. Joan was one of the best friends I ever had, and together with our dear husbands we had many marvellous adventures, travels and experiences.

When I think of Joan I remember those beautiful lines from *A Course in Miracles* – 'In me is love perfected, fear impossible and joy established without opposite' – because she was so loving, fearless and joyful.

Joan was that rare combination, a very spiritual person with great insight and compassion and a rich inner life – yet also very grounded, capable, practical and efficient in her work. One poignant example of this was Joan's decision, soon after her diagnosis, to teach Richard to cook during the last months of her life. A person like that is the essence of 'love in action'.

Richard and Joan were always a great team and now Joan the pioneering Aries has gone ahead and Richard the mediating Libran has become a devoted link between the worlds, channelling and producing this book.

What makes the book more than a moving personal story, one that we can engage in and make our own? Firstly, it is full of the great universal principles, ageless wisdom and values, which are at the core of every religion yet above them all. Then, these inspiring concepts are presented afresh in simple and often beautiful words relevant to today's issues.

The central theme of the book is this: connecting often with our inner world and changing our perspective is so powerful that, rather than being overwhelmed with the mad rush of life, we can find a place of peace and happiness within and make an important difference to the world around us.

In this process we will have all the help we need from our spiritual guides who have been with us over many lives, and our loved ones who have gone before us.

Above all, this book is a witness to the power of love to reach out and span the two worlds of earth and spirit. It is a source of encouragement, hope and comfort, especially at times of difficulty or crisis. Realising that none of us is alone or without meaning or support, *that nothing can ever harm the spirit within* and that our lives are eternal can give us the strength and confidence to go forward with new joy and enthusiasm.

Sandra Levy, London

Preface

This book has been written by teachers from the next world. We all, without exception, traverse to the spirit world when our life here on earth has served its purpose and comes to an end. It is only the body that dies for the consciousness, also called soul or spirit, survives so-called death and makes a new home for itself on the other side.

Jesus said 'In my Father's house are many mansions'. The soul is welcomed on arrival before taking up its new life and rightful place, on a level appropriate to the soul's progress, taking into consideration the life just led on earth.

The teachings in this book were transmitted through a channel chosen for this purpose and it will be explained later how it all came about. It has been a truly successful experience enjoyed by souls on both sides of the divide. We have been inspired to place the teachings in a certain order and it is recommended that they are not read as a normal book but, rather, on a daily or ad hoc basis so that the maximum effect may be received by the reader. You may find there are similarities in the various articles but, on a deeper level, each is important in its own way.

We wish you special experiences within as you read, contemplate and meditate on the words.

Introduction

There is a great need today in the world for peace and understanding between all men and women. There have been times in the earth's history when radical physical changes have taken place because moral and other living conditions declined to shockingly low levels. We now seem to be heading toward another catastrophe unless changes in our thinking, outlook and way of life come soon.

Selfishness and accumulation of money appear to be the goal in commercially and financially developed countries, whereas just providing food for the family in so-called underdeveloped countries becomes the aim. This imbalance is getting worse as the gulf between the two extremes becomes wider.

Wars and political arguments continue to have prominence, as do mass crimes, increasing leisure drug experimentation and exploitation of the world's natural resources. Bickering and infighting within and between religious organisations has also become more widespread. In certain religions the doctrines and instructions are so rigid that they rarely provide the soul with the freedom to expand its consciousness.

So, taken as a whole, there appears to be a significant need for change on the earth. Straightforward spiritual teachings, taught and shown by example, are offered in this book, received in meditation from some of those gone before us into the next life.

This introduction sets the scene for a collection of inspired teachings that were channelled, recorded and written down. This compilation is therefore offered not as a solution to the world's problems, but as a starting point for those who feel within that something different needs to happen in this beautiful world of ours. As always, in this type of situation, healing and transformation begins with the individual.

Part One

Background

How the Book Came to be Written

Unknown to me the seeds for this book were sown several years ago when my wife, Joan Brake, and I had promised each other that whoever passed to the next life first would make every effort to make contact from the other side. I believe Joan's passing was the catalyst for the remarkable events that followed, resulting in this book which my friends and I have been so privileged to produce. Before I tell the story of how it came about I feel I should include some background information.

Joan had always been interested in spirituality and her life was one of service, firstly being a devoted wife and mother to three sons, and then helping her elderly parents. However it wasn't until the 1980s that, together, we became spiritual seekers. Our search took us into Spiritualism, Raja Yoga, Theosophy, Interfaith, 'A Course in Miracles', other philosophies and religious teachings, including visits to Sai Baba at his ashrams in India. We aimed to follow his teachings that included selfless service and the Oneness of all life which we studied for some years.

During this time Joan was actively involved in facilitating spiritual meetings, study groups, weekend retreats and taking groups to India. She also helped in food kitchens for the homeless, day centres for the elderly, horse riding for special needs children and was the instigator for a new local Gateway Junior Club. All this she undertook with love, enthusiasm and boundless energy.

A few months after Joan's passing in February 2012, I felt inspired to write down thoughts. These usually came into my mind when I was about to go to bed, or sometimes when I was actually in bed. These jottings became letters to and from Joan. I believe these letters originated on a soul level as the tone and quality demonstrated that I could not have written them in my normal conscious state. They were far too good for my standard of writing and came through quickly, unlike my usual slow letter writing speed.

There have been over one hundred letters since the first one on 20 June 2012 and, although the frequency has now reduced, they are still being received. I also heard from Joan through a medium last summer, when it was confirmed that I was receiving letters from the next world.

One morning, about a month later, in meditation, something in me started to receive words in the form of teachings which I wrote down. I was later inspired to transfer the articles, short at first, to a computer. Most mornings I received these inspirational words and before long there was a collection of twenty to thirty.

One day there was mention of a new project and from then on the writings became longer and were certainly not written by my normal self. Again, the quality and speed of channelling told me that the inspiration came from the other side. A subsequent letter from Joan revealed that the teachings were given by a group of wise souls, including a former Chinese healer and philosopher, an Italian monk and a North American Indian and herself. Later they gave themselves the collective name of Joyful One which helped to ensure there were no emotional feelings within individuals during the channelling. Joyful One is a very suitable name as they so often portray happiness, joy and sense of humour in their messages.

At the same time I was also receiving writings, from the same source, calling me 'my boy'. They contained advice for me, intermingled with more teachings with the result that I then had three folders containing letters, teachings and advice.

By now I was using a recorder to ease the way in transcribing these beautiful teachings into the written word. Certain of the articles were sent to various friends with positive results. They confirmed that the teachings were special and not in my imagination. I was encouraged by them and others, including my spirit friends, to put the articles together as a collection of teachings in a book.

Later I was inspired to invite my good friends, Jan and Brian, to sit with me in a circle once a week, and the extra energy from the three of us facilitated a smoother transmission for the additional teachings. One teaching received in this way was from the higher realms and is included later in the appendix. Jan and Brian were already assisting in proofreading the material leaving me to concentrate on the channelling and preparing the first reading of the articles.

It was confirmed to us during a circle meeting that the articles were to be produced as a book and that many like-minded people, around the world, will be brought together and inspired to live a more spiritual life.

At this point one may well think that these letters could be attributed to the imagination of a husband coming to terms with being a widower. Believe me, I questioned this many times and when the teaching articles began I questioned even more.

Today I have no doubt as to the integrity of these teachings; they speak for themselves, and I, and my friends, have willingly undertaken to bring this book to publication.

Part Two

Early Writings

Universal Love

Love is the strongest force in existence. It emanates from God and has its form in all of creation throughout the physical universe and, of course, in unseen universes. It is the power that maintains regular movement of celestial bodies, while here on earth it is responsible for all of nature, including the seasons, the tides, the various mineral, vegetable, animal kingdoms and mankind.

This love force is what scientists are looking for to confirm the interconnectedness, Oneness, of all life. They don't realise that God is not only in all mankind but also in the smallest cell on the earth and the universe.

How, then, can this knowledge be understood and applied to everyday life as we know it?

Well, it explains the Bible saying that God is aware of the tiniest sparrow falling out of the air and knowing each hair on the human head.

When people know this and, more importantly, understand the meaning of it they will wonder at the enormity of it all. They will be crestfallen that they have bickered and argued over the smallest divisions which have, in some cases, escalated to war. How can people argue over ownership of land, countries, etc. when only God really owns everything and all is held in His hand?

The answer lies within each individual when he or she realises and experiences the Oneness of all life: that is the love within all mankind and all species, even within the earth itself. Then we shall truly begin to see the New Age and heaven on earth.

This teaching has been handed down for centuries by true Masters and Avatars, but man has generally chosen to ignore it. Instead he thinks he knows better and gets caught up in the material side of life, forgetting the spiritual aspect.

Therefore, mankind now has a tremendous opportunity to use

this knowledge from the scientists and put into practice the philosophy of God's universal love for all His creation by loving his fellow man and all life.

We will see small facets and groups putting this into practice until, with great expansion, man's love for God and his fellow man become so widespread that the whole world becomes engulfed in the new Golden Age.

The Now

What you have done is of no consequence to the *now*, that ever present now in which all is held.

My friends, this is the most important teaching that can be given because the now contains everything and nothing. Love, the greatest energy, is contained in the now. Everything emanates from the now so take time to relish it and feel the peace of the now. Stay a moment in silence, for that also is the now.

So, what is the basis of the now? It is the I AM of all creation, the I AM of pre-creation and the I AM of post-creation. In other words All That Is is contained in the very moment of now.

All time comes out of the now and all things will return to the now. All great ideas and inventions, all great works of art and inspiration arise out of the now. Take time, my friends, to *be*, to be in the now for the now holds everything. The now is a single moment continuing to infinity but can be lost by thinking of the future or past, instead of living in the now. Everything arises and returns to the now, so be in the now always and all will be well.

This is the greatest teaching for mankind today.

Inspiration

Inspiration is the platform for real communication from within. When you need answers to problems, be they personal or work-related, you say you sleep on it and you know what to do in the morning. Where do you think this inspiration comes from?

Well, you could say the brain but that is only the tool to relate the answer: it can only work with the information given to it, like a computer. You could say your higher self or soul and this would be nearer the truth.

Inspiration comes from God through various channels, via the soul, and is best achieved when the thought process is still, when asleep or when lost in work, recreation or meditation, for example.

So, the clearer the mind the easier it is to receive. It may not be a dramatic answer and may just be a nudge to make contact with someone in need, but the more open the channel the easier it is to receive the communication.

Slide

You see a slide and you think down is the only way. Why should it be? There are all manner of ways to go if you will just concentrate within. Why do we only think of going down or staying the same, why not change our attitude and think of going upwards into higher realms?

Why do so many people resist change? It is the easy road to follow but growth only comes when change is welcomed with a pure heart, ready and willing to embrace the future with confidence. Look into your very beings and feel if this is correct, then think positively when meeting new challenges and your whole self will embrace a totally new exciting outlook on life.

Think of Me

I love you wherever you are, and whenever you need Me I am there. The sun melts the ice and I melt the hearts that are open and ready.

Think of Me constantly and I will protect and guide you through life. There is no need to fall on your knees or prostrate yourself on the floor. Just think of Me in your meditation, in the quiet of your heart in the middle of a busy day. In fact anytime you think of Me I am there. You go about your daily chores, sometimes so busy that you don't have time to go within.

So think of Me, feel Me in your heart and together we will change the world, not by becoming a leader of nations but by being your real self, the self that can do anything. Start with yourself, this will then reflect on your family. Then your neighbourhood, your village, your town, your country and eventually the whole world will be aware of the love, peace and truth that is available to them when they are ready to receive it.

Your slightest smile, loving action, or gift to others has abundant results as it snowballs to so many. Don't think you have nothing to give as all have My precious love within, and as you give more so shall your heart expand to give love everywhere you go.

Part Three

General Observations on Life

The Human Race

Today we would like to say a few words about the human race, not only as you know it now, but also as it was in the days of Jesus 2000 years ago.

There was an abundance of good vegetation, unspoilt by chemicals, on the land and in the rivers. The food grown contained higher levels of nutrients, as did the meat and fish which formed much of the diet in those days. Drought, floods and desert areas happened then, just as now, and the weather was affected by man's treatment of the land, animals and people around him.

There were, even in those days, rich and poor people; living conditions having varied according to where, and into which family, you were born. It was easy then for the soul to decide, with help from those in spirit, where to incarnate on earth.

This is still the same for those incarnating today, and you may ask why the population is at its highest level ever and set to increase at an alarming rate. The answer to this, of course, is that it is all in the Divine plan. However, there are contributory factors in that the earth is such a special spiritual training ground, with so many conditions and different cultures that these experiences cannot be obtained anywhere else. The evolution and predicted opportunities now, and in the immediate future, mean that souls are literally waiting for their chance to incarnate here again. Of course there are also a large number of new souls incarnating at this time which helps to create, shall we say, a time bomb of quite extraordinary conditions.

Seen from our eyes your time on earth is only a blip in the magnitude of eternal life but, we appreciate from our own past experiences, this does not feel the case for you all at this time of your current sojourn. Needless to say you have such a variety of old and new souls, and those in-between, that life is guaranteed to be full and ever-changing as the earth and its people evolve at an ever-increasing rate.

The saying 'stop the bus, I want to get off' applies to so many people today as they can't keep up with all the latest inventions and ever more complicated, politically correct, government rules and regulations. In the midst of all this industrial and commercial growth there are some who drop out of the rat race, finding modern conditions all too difficult for them. Of course there are still areas, ever-dwindling, where a life spent away from all the hustle and bustle of normal life can still exist and those who choose this find their peace and solitude. For the rest, you wonder where it will all end as the natural resources are being used up at a rapid rate and, in certain parts of the world, climate is having a devastating effect on crops.

So, you can see from our perspective conditions are perfect for soul growth and the difficulties you all experience from time to time are necessary and planned. The opportunities for willing souls to help bring in the New Age are enormous and much has already been achieved both here, and on the earth, to prepare for the changes.

We, therefore, say to people, live according to your heart's dictates and you will create an oasis within the mad rush of human life, where more and more people can rest and take refuge, so that they may be re-invigorated to bring about the marvels of the New Age.

Everyone has a purpose in life and also a time to explore it so that the earth and its people will evolve into the next wondrous stage according to the Divine plan.

When you find your peace you will be ready to live by example and give out God's love in all you do, wherever you go and to whoever you meet. Be full of confidence then that all is as it should be and you are all playing your part in the grand plan for this planet.

Nature

The Son of God is present in your hearts when you open up to the Oneness of all life. Today, instead of being in a forest of trees you are in a jungle of concrete in your towns and cities. The air is polluted not only with toxic fumes but also with an enormity of radio waves. Your fields are full of insecticides and artificial fertilisers which find their way into the rivers and, subsequently, into the great oceans where all aquatic life has been affected. Now, your scientists have been growing genetically modified crops and wonder why nature is rebelling by creating so-called super weeds and insects.

While your scientists have been helped with new inventions as part of the earth's evolvement, money and some not so good intentions have sent several of those inventions off track. The result is that what you call nature is fighting to restore the equilibrium that God originally created.

It is, therefore, good to reflect upon the glories of nature with such beauties as sunsets, and waters reflecting the sun and moon. God's natural laws ensure everything in the world, like the tides, the moon's and earth's orbits for example, work to an exact timing and movement that is incredible to the human mind. The balance of life on your earth is very delicate and can be upset by man's greed and with his relationship with his fellow man. This is happening now and the results can be seen and felt by your changing ecology and climate.

It requires men and women to realise what is happening to nature, and to a certain extent this has occurred, but green issues and plans on their own will not solve the problems. They go far deeper into today's way of life where most people want more and more and only the few find unconditional giving to be the norm.

Much is made of the current state of the earth and efforts are being made in some quarters to improve the situation. However, a radical change in the spiritual side of life is required to form changes within before we see a snowballing effect on life in general. There are individuals and groups working toward this end, but they are very much the exception. Until there is a fundamental change in people's desires and expectations, with a readiness to accept that we are all God's children, brothers and sisters, unconditional love will not be restored to this world.

More and more people are aware of the need for change within themselves and we are working with those people, whether they know it or not, to bring about the right conditions and foundations, both for an inward look and, also, for them to take a step back and look at their own lives. It is, therefore, important that certain people lead the way, by example, to change their own lives and thus the lives of others as their friends and acquaintances see the inward and outward effects showing in their faces and in their actions.

First of all then an acceptance of the need for change is necessary by individual questioning and giving positive thought to do something about their lives. A start has been made: there are people ready and willing to play their part in this fundamental restructuring of life's basic tenets, so it is a good time to be sure that, with God in their hearts, a revolution in the minds of people to live a new way of life will take place.

The Search

There is a time for everyone when they wonder what this life is all about, what it is for and why they are here. It is at this point in time that they are vulnerable to any attractive train of thought that might be 'in' at that moment. It happens to people from all different backgrounds and religions and those with no religion.

What causes this self-analysis in man to come to the fore? It can often be a trauma in life, such as an accident, bereavement or break-up in a relationship; or it can simply be that the soul is ready for an awakening of some description.

There are plenty of openings available to the searcher through books, word of mouth and the internet. Help is given from this side of life, when the person is ready, to point them in the right direction. These days there are various groups and spiritual organisations, even religious sects, which play their part in helping the person to obtain answers to their questions.

There are meetings ranging from clairvoyance to full enlighten-ment and many life-changing courses are available, so there is usually one appropriate for each person who is ready for their journey.

It may appear to be a sudden decision, but is usually a gradual change in the pattern of one's social and business directions, resulting in a change of thoughts about one's life. This culminates one day in a decision to find out more about life's eternal mysteries.

The soul will recognise the teachings that appeal to it with a knowing in the heart when he or she feels ready to pursue a certain pathway. There is a keenness to learn more and chase after lectures and reading material until they take stock of where they are and what they need to do next.

They often meet like-minded people and are able to progress together as their search continues. There comes a point where they feel unconditional love and peace and some have an overwhelming feeling of Oneness. There is then a knowing that God exists for them in whatever way they imagine and, from then on, they can experience remarkable so-called coincidences and, sometimes, small miracles. They become transformed into giving service to communities, whether within a group or individually, and life has real meaning for them at last and they have a form of happiness not felt before.

As more and more people feel the urge to search for life's answers the need for teachers and facilitators will become greater and coordinators, to bring it all together, will be found to be available.

Look deep into your hearts, my friends, and be ready when the call comes to take on these responsibilities, as you are led by us to be in the right place at the right time to follow your chosen pathway.

You will know when conditions are ready for you to make this leap into the unknown, and you will not be alone as the Great Spirit is guiding your every step as you embark on this exciting and rewarding new way of life.

Be ready then, my friends, for the call within as you climb the steps to your newfound freedom, and your pathway opens up before you in ways undreamed of and the love within you drives you ever forward to new feelings of love and ecstasy.

You will never look back once you have found the longings of the heart and spirit within and, as you climb to new heights, you will know the work you will be destined to do as we all come together in proclaiming the arrival of the New Age.

Peace

Love conquers all ills and adverse conditions in human life. When unconditional love is given, or received, there is no room for any negativity.

Take peace then and let the mind dwell on its beauty and strength, where all positive thoughts and actions stem from. Once the mind becomes peaceful there is an all-encompassing effect on the body where all its cells create a calming throughout it. All negative emotions, such as anger, envy, worry and other distractions, are dispelled.

Going into deep peace within leads to a change in the alpha waves of the brain and allows for a fresh healing within the body that has more beneficial sustenance than sleep.

Peace is contagious and can immediately be felt when meeting someone in this glorious state. Once this deep peace is felt it leads to contentment beyond belief within, and without, the human being. The cells are rejuvenated and a bright light comes from within to create a glow felt, if not seen, by other people. Once this state of peace occurs an equilibrium, stretching out to the extremities of the aura, takes place and will change forever the personality and life of the individual.

An inward knowing that all life is One is acknowledged and it takes over as an incredible bliss ensues throughout the entity. In this state one feels God's unconditional love within all life, and truth, knowledge and wisdom is attained.

This, of course, may be called enlightenment, to which all souls are leading, and it simply means being completely at One with All That Is, the Great White Spirit or whatever description one chooses of God.

I give you peace then, my friends, peace that passes all understanding.

Light

Do you see the light?

My friends, this is such an important question with more than one meaning. Generally it means do you understand, or is there a light that you can see, but we mean the light and love that is within all of us.

This light appears slowly at first but, as one becomes open to more than just physical life on the surface, then it becomes brighter. The more one gives out love in service to one's fellow man the more it grows. Many people are unaware of this light within as they are so busy in life and are distracted by modern appliances.

However, for those who make time to sit quietly and meditate, sending out loving and healing thoughts, then the light can be seen within and it becomes brighter the more time one spends with the inner self and the God within.

We are all connected by this light, this Divine light, shining on and in all life. It permeates from the cells through the body and into the aura, where it can be seen by people who have the gift of aura vision. The density of light and the colours of the aura denote so much about the individual character, health, attitude to life, love and relationship with all life. It shows the caring and healing natures and, of course, its giving or selfishness; also the current state of mind.

There are very few people who can read auras, but the light emanating from those souls who are full of love and service to mankind can be felt, if not seen, by people when in their company. It creates a calming effect and people cannot fail to notice a special attraction.

So, my friends, you all have this light within you and, as you develop your understanding of the deeper meaning of life and knowledge of the spiritual side, so shall your light begin to shine brightly and give off this intangible magnetism to all who come in contact with you.

You can close your eyes and see the light within, which appears to grow throughout your inner and outer being, and you may feel in meditation that you are connected to all life with this wondrous feeling of Oneness. This may only happen fleetingly at first, and take many years or even lifetimes to reach this supreme state, but everyone has the ability, if not the desire, to see the light within at some time in their life.

When seen on a regular basis it becomes a guiding light, because intuition often accompanies it when answers to problems and various questions seem to come out of nowhere.

So, take time my friends for quiet periods, however short, in your day and the light within will be of great benefit to not only you but to all who come in contact with you on your wonderful journey of life.

Time

'The Lord hath spoken' says the scriptures, and those who followed the words became the chosen few who, throughout history, have followed God regardless of the consequences.

They felt God within them and were able to live according to their faith without fear or favour, and love their fellow man without question, even when they were ridiculed and could lose their lives. They were usually great teachers, not just with their words but by their actions, being living examples of godly men and women.

How can you live like these people today, with the speed and conditions of modern life? Most people are in such a hurry that they spend very little time, if any, in quiet prayer and solitude during their normal days. When you do take time for this you will find that your life miraculously becomes less hectic, and yet the important things in life still get done without so much pressure.

Your earth time is never really understood and you often comment that it is very fast when you are enjoying life and slow when you are unhappy or depressed. Time was only developed to help manage your days and was never intended to rule your lives. Therefore, use it as a guide only and live according to your heart for you will find then that you have time to fit in everything that matters.

So, live by love and all else follows like clockwork and you will feel fulfilled at the end of the day. We are not saying that life will be like a bed of roses as you will still have problems and issues to deal with, but even these will appear to be less difficult and solved more easily as you follow your life's pathway.

Listen to your heart centre, where your God resides, and you will be inspired to spend your time in service to your fellow men and women. It may be by thought, a word in the right place, teaching or by actions. Whatever it is, you will know what to do or say. Listen within, not necessarily to thoughts or words but also for instinct and feelings.

Therefore, make time in your busy days for contact with your God and, eventually, it will feel like a constant love in your heart, with a knowing of what to do and say without thinking too much.

The Silence

Listen for that still small voice in the silence of your heart. As you get used to silence it becomes like a refuge in the middle of your busy days. Once you hear this voice, and it becomes a regular occurrence, you will find it is easier to go into that silence which is a God-given sanctuary.

Many people are frightened of, or do not like, the silence, especially these days when everything is so noisy and people even use earphones when walking, jogging or cycling. What are people frightened of in the silence; are they frightened of themselves or what the silence will reveal?

People have forgotten the art of being alone with their thoughts and, instead, accompany themselves with noise. It seems the only time people are really quiet is when they go to sleep and even then there may be a TV or radio on in the bedroom. No wonder their dreams are often nightmarish, as dreams can be affected by the noisy happenings of the day.

Look at someone with peace shown in their face and mannerisms, rare these days, and it is almost certain that they treasure their silent times. It is like so many things in life, the thought of what may happen is often the opposite, or different, to what actually happens. Thus so with the silence: people would expect it to be a waste of time and difficult to deal with when, in fact, it can be the most peaceful and beautiful time in one's life.

It is not necessary to recite many prayers when going into the silence, although some people find it helps them. Just try to release all thoughts and feelings from your mind and breathe slowly as your whole body relaxes. It can be just for a few seconds to begin with and, as one gets used to it, the time spent in this way will probably increase to become a regular occurrence.

Each of us have different needs and will experience differing reactions, but we say that everyone will benefit from going into the silence regularly as that is where you meet your real self or the God centre. Hence the feelings of peace and love will grow in you as you become proficient at finding the deep silence.

These experiences will then be reflected in your ways; you will become less agitated and find that problems become less severe as your whole demeanour changes.

You may not notice much change at first but, as you continue, you will find your relationships become stronger and less stressful. Other people will notice a difference in you, not outwardly at first but generally in your overall manner, as your self-assurance and tolerance come to the fore in your life. It will also become much easier to find time for those quiet solitary sessions as a warm glow and light fills your whole being.

Therefore, my friends, it doesn't cost anything other than your time and the rewards you reap will be beyond your wildest dreams.

Living in the Now

It is in the now when all things happen. That glorious moment that can seem to last forever or be so fleeting that it is gone before it is realised.

How can one be aware of the now because most things are thought, done, or just happen without any awareness in the matter? It is a moment in time when one can be at One with God and All That Is. Why should you even want to be aware of this moment in your busy lives? Well, my friends, it is because your lives can be transformed both physically and spiritually by being aware, living in it and by it, as the now is the heart of peace, love and all your thoughts and actions as you make yourself conscious of it within.

For centuries, man has endeavoured to find the secret of life by prayer, meditation, yoga and, yes, by science, but the secret is found by living in the now. This is achieved by stopping for a moment and dwelling in the now, which will last as long as you want it to if you stay in that certain *being*. You can live the rest of your life from there, always being subconsciously aware of it in the background as you go about your daily activities.

It is not something that just happens but, once felt, you will want to experience it again. The best way to bring yourself back to this during your busy day is to pause and feel the now in what you are doing. We realise you can't drop everything, while you are in the middle of something, but you can think of that individual moment and be aware of it every so often. As this becomes a habit, and especially when you do this in your prayer and quiet times, you will find yourselves wanting to be in the *instant* and have the goodwill feeling within. In time this will not become something you make yourself do: it will be automatic and, eventually, always be there.

This can take years or only moments to happen depending upon your wish and determination. What can be said by those who actually live in the now is that they have enduring happiness, which is shown on their faces and in their thoughts and actions. They automatically know what to do in difficult situations and find their lives are completely fulfilled as they become living examples of love and peace in this day and age.

New Day

How wonderful is this new day; a unique, blank sheet ready to be filled with the glories of God.

Whether it be spent outside or at home it will be unlike any that have gone before. You may feel your life is humdrum and unchanging but if you look at yourself, and what you are experiencing, you will notice differences. For example, think how you felt yesterday and the day before at the same time. If you are honest with yourself you will admit that, for no apparent reason, some days you feel on top of the world and on others you may feel depressed and lonely with all the difficulties of life on your shoulders. On other days you may feel in-between these extremes but, however you feel, it will have a bearing on how you experience your day.

There are so many factors that affect your day which might be exciting and a time of great anticipation, or it may be the opposite when you are dreading the thought of the day ahead. As you age your outlook on life often changes; one is said to be wiser, for example, and such things as education can alter the way you look at life.

Some people spend their day rushing around, visiting lots of people in different areas, and others stay in one place, be it their home, care home or hospital, etc. The result is the same, wherever you are, in that your new day, every second of it, is unique to you and a great gift from God. To see it from this point of view enables you to look differently at everything that is before you. Realising this can change your attitude to life and, in many cases, can lead to a connection or reconnection with your inner being so that the path ahead becomes something to explore with a keenness and excitement not seen before. You may still be concerned with certain things that have to be done in your day but, coming from this perspective, the eventual experience will not normally be as bad as feared.

So, how can you live your life with a keen anticipation and zest for it? Look at yourselves and realise that God is within, then connect to that vital heart centre throughout the day and you will feel the peace of the moment, which leads to a newfound confidence and knowing as the day unfolds. Some people literally hand over their lives to God, their thoughts, feelings and actions and they will receive the same feeling of well-being.

It is really all about realising that it is not just the body living this life but the trinity of mind, body and spirit bringing them all into harmony with one another. When you are in this wonderful state your life will change forever: you will have a permanent glow about you as you bring your blessings to bear on all you meet.

Then, when you look back on your day you will feel fulfilled and enriched with the satisfaction of knowing it has been well and truly lived.

The Life Force

Abseiling is something undertaken by few people as it appears dangerous to come down the side of a building, say, on a rope. In fact it is safe providing the anchorage points, and the rope itself, are strong.

This can be compared to one's attitude to life when putting oneself in the hands of others to ensure a safe result. A good anchorage, or foundation, is essential in life to give confidence as one learns the abilities to live from day-to-day. So, what is this anchorage or foundation? It is love, the life force given to us by God that enables the human body to operate and grow. You may have had a difficult childhood or a perfect one but the love within is the same for all. God does not pick and choose to whom to give His love and it is up to each one how to use it. Just as a strong rope and anchorage are essential for abseiling so is God's love essential for life as you know it.

The majority of people are not aware of this love, or life force, as they assume the body works by itself when it receives air, drink and food. Even doctors, in general, do not believe, or are not aware, that life would not happen without God's will. What makes the lungs breathe when you are asleep or the heart to pump blood around the body?

Most people assume it all works on its own as that is what it appears to do. So, if you are dependent upon God for your life wouldn't it be sensible to recognise this and thank Him in your prayers and quiet times? You would then be in contact with your Maker, and literally feel the life force within as you come close to that wondrous power. However you picture your God know that this power is within all of you and, when called upon, is always ready and willing to respond.

Once you relate to your God within on a regular basis you will begin to experience that all-encompassing peace and Oneness, as feelings of bliss become more prevalent in your life.

New Year Opportunity

Flexibility in all one's thoughts and actions results in the body adapting to changing conditions of life on earth. When people have a fixed, unbending attitude to life they are susceptible to all kinds of ill health and tend to be tense most of the time.

The body is supposed to be supple with the ability to move like a ballet dancer. It is born like this and, as such, is often able to avoid injuries from falls, whereas at the other end of the scale older people tend to break bones more easily at their time of life. A life of stress is a major contributory factor in the general phenomena of disease. The body has a natural reaction to fear, for example, going back to its early days on earth. However, it was never intended that the body should be in a permanent state of readiness for reactions to problems, which is why so many people appear to be continually stressed.

Modern life with its non-ending communicative activities leaves the body unable to relax between tasks. It appears to be continually on edge, causing an excess of chemicals or hormones, such as adrenalin, to be produced. No wonder many countries have become known as nations of pill poppers to combat the effects of the out-of-balance bodies. These pills then cause their own side effects and a sad merry-go-round starts with further pills needed to counteract the new side effects.

Where will it all end? Oh! My friends, what has all this so-called progress in the modern world produced? A plethora of diseases, ever-increasing, and as one is eradicated others replace it and so on.

The body, mind and spirit has its own mechanism for healing but all three need to be in harmony to create the balance necessary for this to take place. Yes, the body system is a magnificent specimen for healing itself if it is given a chance. Why do you think you sometimes take to your beds to recover from certain ailments? Because it gives the body a chance to put its own healing devices into action, while the stress of modern life is removed for a while.

Your bodies were not intended to suffer diseases and the answer lies in the word disease itself. A New Year, with many people making New Year resolutions, is an ideal time to take stock of one's life and take the opportunity to rebalance it by remembering that one is, in fact, spirit with a body and not the other way around. So, how do you use this information to harmonise your spirit, mind and body? Take the time or, should we say, make the time for relaxation away from all outside influences, not in the sense of a holiday, although of course that would be beneficial, but in your crowded normal day. Stop everything momentarily and bring yourself into balance. This can be for just a second to start with and, then, gradually increasing its regularity until your day becomes interspersed with these beautiful moments when the body becomes in tune and the healing process starts from within.

You all have the potential to experience these healing moments in your own way and, by keeping to this regime, your life will become transformed, enabling full balance to return with all the benefits associated with it.

New Age Vibrations

Great is the time coming when all peoples will sit down together in peace without the need to hold talks for peace, which invariably fail anyway. It will be natural for them to live this way for the world, my friends, will change as the New Age becomes reality.

So much has been talked about the New Age for what seems to be a long time but it is only like a blink in the eye of God. Many of you have been looking for signs of this New Age, through outward conditions and man's relationship with man, but things seem to be getting worse worldwide, both economically and with man's greed still very much to the fore.

However, the vibrations of the world began to increase during the last decade and, this year, they will continue at a much faster rate with the effects starting to be felt in all four corners of the globe. It will not result in little green men from space scrambling all over the place, nor will just the chosen few be left to start a new race on earth. No, as you would expect, changes will be a little more subtle as people, unknowingly, will pick up on these changes and will undergo a type of lifting, a lightness in their minds and bodies, as these new conditions are produced by their inherent spiritual natures.

Then, a more intense quest for spiritual knowledge will begin to emerge. This will not be so much through organised religions, as their traditions, creeds and rules will restrict the natural flow of development, but mainly through small groups receiving the knowledge and wisdom necessary to spread the New Age spiritual philosophies in a manner understood by the general public.

While all this is going on people will at last feel there is more to life than money and attaining more luxuries. They will want to know, for example, what life is all about, the reason that they are here, what happens to them after death and how to achieve real happiness.

The result will be a change in feelings with a more friendly and loving attitude to their fellow man. They will look after each other more in terms of family, neighbours, work colleagues and even people who were not exactly enemies but certainly not friends either. This new caring attitude, 'love in action', will spread through communities, on to governments and gradually across the earth as people are prepared to start trusting one another again.

We know all this sounds like Utopia, and it will not happen all at once, but the foundations have, and are, being put into place for growth of the spiritual aspect of life through people and groups in all lands. A growing thirst for knowledge and wisdom will be felt among all people, and no longer will governments continue to resort to wars and strong-arm tactics to resolve problems as people will no longer accept these policies. As this love in action snowballs and reaches gigantic proportions the new Golden Age will truly be ushered in with all the wonders that a lasting peace in the world, both among people and nations, will bring. Nature will once more settle down and people will look after and tend the environment, instead of exploiting it as has been the case for so long.

Well, my friends, this may seem like a fairy tale but, we assure you, it is in the Divine plan that the vibrational changes taking place will have the desired effect for man to eventually live in peace with his fellow man and for the long-sought-after Golden Age to finally happen.

I AM That

'I AM That' is such a powerful statement that most people will not understand its meaning. The 'I AM' is the God within and the additional word 'That' emphasises the meaning.

I AM That, said in silence, invokes a centring of one's being into the most beautiful peace where the body itself pays homage to its master. If said or thought repeatedly an amazing healing process begins as one is aware of the beauties within which extend to the Oneness of all life. The peace that descends upon the mind expands throughout the body and to all surroundings, including the very air you breathe and the objects and life within your vicinity.

This saying, or mantra, is very powerful and can be used at any time in any conditions and can be particularly useful to people if they have problems or need direction in their lives. I AM That said with faith can change one's life as its effects are felt both in the short-term and the long-term. The special feelings involved within when repeating the mantra can lead to finding one's real pathway, as the still small voice will become more prominent, leading to truths and knowledge not previously experienced.

Words and phrases can be very powerful and can affect the well-being or otherwise of the individual, depending upon what is said or thought. So, if one has been surrounded by negative thoughts and words, for example, it can leave one deflated and in need of sustenance. By repeating I AM That equanimity will be restored quickly, and conditions in you and your surroundings will show a remarkable change.

Therefore, my friends please remember that selecting a phrase or mantra appropriate to you, and using it, can be one of the most rewarding experiences in life today. It can be used in any circumstances, from a peaceful one to an angry or confrontational one, and is the best antidote for any stressful situation when said in truest faith and sincerity.

All's Well that Ends Well

You are familiar with the term 'All's well that ends well' and this indicates a positive attitude to something that finished satisfactorily but had difficulties or problems on the way. Human life is rather like this: it usually starts well and in the normal run of events ends in old age when it has had the chance to be at peace with itself before the end. In-between there is usually an eventful life full of experiences and memories, some of which can be treasured while others are better forgotten.

The journey of life is so important and little moments are often ignored, especially in earlier days, as one tends to be always thinking and planning the future rather than enjoying and living the moment to the full. In the other extreme, when getting toward the end of life, one tends to be looking back on memories instead but, in both cases and most of the time in-between, the art of living in the moment seems to be lost on people. This tends to be exacerbated today with all the modern inventions for saving time, etc. that life apparently moves much faster than days of old. This, of course, is all in the mind as time is the same as it always has been and it is the beholder who determines how fast or slow it goes. The faster one moves and is caught up in the drive for ever-increasing productivity, not just at work but in life generally, the more dramatic is the resultant life where there never appears to be time for the mind and body to relax and recuperate.

Where is all this leading and what can be done to change this type of life where there is no time to smell the roses and enjoy the journey, rather than be taken along for the ride? It is time to stop and look at oneself before the body reacts, stopping itself through illness or accident in order to achieve the same end. Much better then to look at one's own life first before it is forced upon one. When was the last time you looked inwardly at your own life? Yes, these questions and thoughts bring one into that zone when everything pauses for a moment or two before one rejoins all the pressures which are so evident in modern-day life. So, look at yourself, do you like what you see? Give yourself time to look at life anew and at ways to change this lifestyle; a time to look within to discover the real you that will help you to adjust your pace of life and possibly point you in a new direction.

Take time to love yourself, that is to love who you *really* are and not who you *think* you are. You are actually mind, body and spirit and by giving yourself time to appreciate this will, by itself, start to bring all three into balance. Then, when you make a habit of introspective pauses, meditations, you will find your life becoming more peaceful with less stress and you will appear to have more time, rather than less, to do the important things in life.

So, love yourself, your new way of life, and you will find that you will make time for caring and loving your fellow human beings. A new purpose and fulfilment will then be ever present in your life.

Energy

Boundless is the energy within one connected to that profound, endless, eternal energy of the Father. You can all connect to this energy by becoming at one with your inner self, that centre of all strength that has existed forever in the Mind of God. Remember to recharge yourself daily with this bounty that is for everyone alike. All that is required is a humbleness and realisation that all life comes from God, whether it is in the physical or spirit realms.

Those of you who are devoting yourselves to a life of service automatically plug into this energy, which can take you to unheard of and unthought-of areas within yourselves that will prepare you for tasks beyond your normal expectations. So, relax, feel and be at One with All That Is and you will develop this boundless love which accompanies the energy. You will be like a transformer as your beacon of light shines forth before you when you go about your daily work and visitations, be they physical or spiritual.

Essence of Life

As this day unfolds, how much time do you spend thinking about why you are here and who, or what, is behind all life? It is in having these thoughts that you begin to open up yourselves to Almighty God, that indescribable energy and intelligence called Love that permeates through all life.

To become one with all in this life is the same wherever you are, be it in the desert, on the sea or in a busy city centre, for God is just as much in the smallest grain of sand as in the largest mountain or in the deepest ocean, and in all life contained therein.

So, all you need do, my friends, is to go within to discover the mysteries of life, for they are to be found when you are ready. With the vibrations rising on the earth more and more people will question life and its origins: by making yourselves receptive to the inner knowledge you will find the answers you have been searching for.

You will then be ready to meet the challenges of the New Age with courage, fortitude and confidence, but above all with love.

Channelling

To be an open channel all you need is a willingness and keenness to put your normal self aside during the periods involved, be they ten minutes or two hours.

Channelling has been used for centuries as a means of healing and teaching from this side of life and varies in intensity, from someone not realising they are channelling to another in full trance. It is tailored to the personality and strengths of the channeller depending, of course, upon the purpose of the communication. It can be anything from a kind word or passing on information, to regular healing and teachings. It can be inspired words put in writing, or a spoken full discourse where the channel is fully aware of what is being said, or he or she steps aside to let us speak through them.

Training is given from here and may have started in previous lives, but it usually appears to start when one opens oneself to these possibilities through meeting with other people searching for spiritual truths. There will always be a need for channels willing to offer themselves for this demanding work, as it requires regular meditative sessions, often in a group but occasionally on one's own, where the sitter opens his or herself to our world. There is naturally more power generated in a group and these circumstances are required for someone going into full trance, with all the attendant safety measures. In these cases the group as a whole give of themselves so that we can work with the channel to produce the spoken words, which may be in the medium's normal tongue or in the accent and character of the entity coming through.

There is continual development going on from this side of life to help people become good channels, as the requirement has never been as great as now with the vibrational changes occurring on earth. As these changes increase the demand will follow for clear spiritual knowledge and guidance. With more channels becoming available there will be a coming-together of like-minded people into groups all over the world, many under different guises, but all with a common love and willingness to do this work, having been called to be ready at this time for the spiritual transformation of the earth and its peoples.

You may think that this has been going on for many years and you would be right. However, what has happened to date has only been the forerunner of what is to take place. We are indebted to all who have set the ball rolling and, indeed, many who are about to be used have been trained and helped by those who have prepared the way.

You will find that the channels or mediums of today will be brought together by us, in a natural and exciting way, to teach and train others across the lands so that there will be sufficient numbers in place to help bring in the new Golden Age in a blaze of glory.

Knowledge

Knowledge is the key to a change in one's life. Everything can be going well but often something seems lacking. For whatever reason it can't be explained and this apparent lack can begin to affect one's day-to-day activities. It is at this point that questions arise and a search has begun. Therefore, when the soul is ready things and actions start to happen, with a word here or there and books mysteriously put in one's way, so the quest begins.

Whatever one's background, religious or secular, it will not stop the increased craving for knowledge. Once the heart is open the pace of knowledge intake increases, with apparent coincidences happening, so that a pathway starts to open up. Before long you will usually meet like-minded people and be invited to meetings to explore the longings of the heart. Age-old wisdom may be given and you will be attracted to certain teachings which feel true to your heart. These days there are so many ways to satisfy desires in this direction through magazines, the internet, books and word of mouth.

You will be led to your appropriate speciality, through knowledge gained, to completely change your life. It happens to people of all ages at the right time. Someone, often an unlikely one, will surprise you with their knowledge and help with advice and invitations to investigate certain areas of a spiritual nature, which will seem right for you at the time.

Your soul will lead you on to many wonderful and unbelievable experiences and you will wonder why this knowledge is not understood by your compatriots, as it seems that once you have taken this spiritual wisdom on board then all your friends and acquaintances should be given the same opportunity. This is when you are disappointed that the majority have no interest at all and you will start to become a little isolated as your insatiable demand for more of the same will probably not be matched by your families or friends. Your way of life and conduct can also change which, again, will tend to leave you more on your own.

However, you will find new friends who more than compensate for the loss of old ones. As you immerse yourself in your new life there will be no shortages of invitations to explore further your quest for spiritual truths. As you become further engrossed you will find practical ways of putting into practice the fruits of your learning by serving your fellow man in all kinds of ways as you are led to use your gifts, unknown to you just a little while ago. You could then become teachers yourselves, and your pathway will become clear as you join so many in bringing spiritual knowledge to the forefront at this time of great need.

Go forth then, my friends, follow your hearts and inner promptings to join the natural revolution in mankind to create new world thinking as the energies assist you all to bring in the new Golden Age.

Golden Refuge

You are ready to resume this life of dedicating all your actions to God. In doing this you will find that obstacles are removed and doors open up as you tread the lighted road ahead.

You can reach the pinnacle of life when you feel the peace and love within your hearts. It is all a matter of disciplining your life in such a way that you make time to start your day in silence when you communicate with your God within. When you commence your days in this manner your mind and whole body become at one as you embark upon the exciting potential of the new day ahead.

Whatever you feel you need to do hand it over to God and you will find you have clearer insights to the problems and tasks facing you. Relax and take the time necessary to tune mind, body and soul. Your path ahead will open with a glorious inner glow, which can stay with you all day as you top-up, from time to time, your connection within. You don't have to physically lie down or meditate during the day, but simply feel the love within your heart centre as you bring yourself momentarily to that beautiful state of peace therein. You can return there at any time, even in the middle of a heated discussion or argument, when you feel far away from love and peace. By mentally bringing yourself back to that beautiful warmth within, your mind will be helped to settle down again enabling your real self to become uppermost, whatever you may be doing or thinking at the time.

It has been described as the golden light within for, once you have experienced this or something similar appropriate to you, you can return to it at any time. You don't have to sit in isolation or close your eyes during the day to experience this state. It will become automatic as you return your busy mind to this golden refuge. It is free and always available to you, whether you are in the depths of despair, in the heights of happiness or in-between. The more you remember to do this, even for only a fleeting second, the easier it will become in your life and you will have the opportunity to recharge your batteries with that hidden energy of love.

You will find that as you become more adept at this way of life you will appear as a beacon of light to people you meet. They will feed off this love and light and the more you give out, whether realising it or not, even more will be replaced for you cannot store this energy of love. It needs to be continually on the move as the natural law ensures there is always sufficient available for everyone.

So, my friends, continually link in to your inner self and you will find your way easily in this confused world, and as people are attracted to you so you will become a living example of love and peace on earth.

Point of No Return

Mankind is almost at that point of no return where material advances have outstripped spiritual ones. Your inventors, politicians and entrepreneurs have, in the main, made their endeavours for importance, moneymaking and advancement their god instead of bringing a balance from the spiritual side of life.

How, then, can all this be changed? This is where the increase in earth's vibrations will feature, as it will affect all people and allow room in their lives for love. Slowly, at first, it will permeate throughout life and people will wonder what is tugging at their hearts and minds. It will make everyone look at their lives and feel a need to change not only their own but the collective local, national and international future outlook.

At the same time there will be an upsurge in the number of people who have given their lives over to God, as they investigate together the teachings of the great Masters who have gone before them. In all cultures there have been great people, teachers, sages and saints, who have trod the path before them, exploring and recording the great spiritual truths of all time. These people had many followers in their lifetimes and afterwards leaving their knowledge and wisdom for all to find. Now is the time for everyone to become hungry for this knowledge as they see their lives are lacking in purpose and direction.

So, my friends, you who have already found that essence in life, missing for so many, will be needed to show the world that there is an inner side to life, where love is paramount and where one can live by the dictates of the heart instead of the mind. You will come to the fore as the great majority of the population start their own inevitable search for that which is *within* and not without. It will start very slowly and people won't realise it is happening, but, as this longing for something else in life grows, new teachings will evolve through you who have been prepared for it. Although the teachings will be based on the age-old wisdom of the Masters it will be presented in such a way that it will be immediately acceptable, and appropriate, for these modern times.

So, we say to those of you who know in your heart of hearts that you have been chosen for this work, listen to your inner being and follow those promptings to prepare yourselves in your own unique ways for the tasks ahead. There are many of you that have started the preparation and are helping others with this work. Therefore, keep in touch by prayer and meditation as a growing force, led from God within, brings you out into the open.

The growing need for this knowledge will be met by those living in love and peace and the promised changes will well and truly have begun in earnest.

Golden Ray

You are in the middle of a Golden Ray which is being adapted along with a change to the vibrations on the earth. The Golden Ray contains love, peace and truth and has been linked to the earth for eons. It is being adjusted and improved in conjunction with the other rays, the colours of which you would recognise from a rainbow.

These rays have always surrounded the earth and they are being strengthened to assist the physical and spiritual aspects of your world. It has become depleted with the exploitation, by man's greed, of the great treasures within its crust. It is not readily known that the minerals and metals are there to assist the whole aura of the earth. While certain ones were meant for man's evolution they were not expected to be extracted in such alarming quantities, leaving denigration of the earth's crust in certain areas. The same thing has been happening with your oceans where trawlers have been built ever larger, to leave the fish stocks so dangerously low that other marine life is struggling to survive.

Therefore, these stronger beautiful rays will be sent to coincide with the increased vibrations and will assist in the regeneration of the earth's seas and crust. However, this cannot take place without a similar increase in the spiritual vibrations, both for the earth and its peoples; they, too, having generally suffered by man's relationship with man and the environment.

Those of you who are sensitive will be assisting with this transformation and will notice a gradual lighter feeling within your bodies, and on the earth's surface, resulting in the purifying of your minds and bodies. This will become noticeable over varying times, as appropriate to your own pathways. Don't worry if you don't experience these changes immediately as the preparation has been going on for an age and the implementation will take another age to complete.

Nevertheless, you are all here at the right time to assist in one way or another in the foundation being laid for this extraordinary and exciting time in the world's history. You may not all notice the subtle change yourselves and, indeed, you may not be aware of how you are involved in these challenging times, but you will still have your part to play.

You will gradually see a change in everyday life as the teachings will be extended across the globe, and more and more of you will feel the call to join the introduction of this amazing love crusade, which will announce the real start to the new Golden Age.

Judgements

Judgement occurs all too readily nowadays with the news being read continually on TV and radio, giving rise to judging all and sundry so much of the time. How often do you judge during the day? If you stopped to count we are sure you would be very surprised. Anything from driving to merely thinking can start it, and making snap judgements at work, or play, is a regular process.

Most judgements are made without knowing both sides of the story and, therefore, reflect badly on the person making that judgement. Indeed, under the natural law of cause and effect this will rebound in some form or other in the future.

Everybody makes judgements and, even when trying not to, one can be put in an unenviable position when being asked directly for a comment on someone else's actions. Even a positive response is still a judgement.

Judgement is at the base of all disharmony and controversy in life today and often leads to more serious disagreements, bad feeling and even feuds. So, how can one start to eradicate it from one's own life? As we have said, it is happening continuously and you would even be judged yourself if you refused to give an opinion on someone. However, when we realise and accept that we are all part of God then this could immediately stop, because you would not want to think you were judging God. This is all very well for those who accept this as fact, and it is still difficult for them, but you would say it is a non-starter for those who didn't believe they were all part of God.

So, some other reason must be found to stop judging, and the answer seems to be in thinking how you would feel by being unfairly judged yourselves. Obviously nobody would want that and so it is a matter for discipline and self-development. Everyone is in this life together and a positive, friendly atmosphere, without judgement, is good for community relations, whether it be in the family, at work, in sport or recreation and, of course, between friends and acquaintances.

It can be such a small thing at first, to resist judging, but the consequences can be quite extensive. Therefore, start in a small way, every day, to avoid giving opinions on people and their activities, and the habit of a lifetime will be broken. The resultant atmosphere in the workplace, etc. will be dramatically improved and it will become a pleasure and joy again to go about one's daily activities.

I in You and You in Me

'I in you and you in Me.' Where have you heard this before? Yes, from all the great Masters for they spoke the truth that all is One and there is no separation. Wherever we are, on your side of life or here, there is no separation. It has always been so and the name given to this truth nowadays is non-duality.

All life, while appearing separate from without, is all One within and the overpowering Oneness can be experienced in the silence and stillness of the heart. We are all connected by the Spirit, this intangible connectedness of love within all beings, which goes right to the very core of your cells.

This truth, above all, demonstrates God and His creation. It explains once and for all that God, in His wisdom, decided to create all life at the start of time so that He, through us, could love Himself.

We are all connected by love, that Divine power forever within us, often remaining stagnant until we are ready to experience the fullness of life, and not just material separateness. You will normally experience the Oneness gradually at first, until it feels that it is opening forth through and out of your bodies. Some people never have this experience, others only tentatively, and just a few have the full flow of love, for and within all, as the connection becomes overriding.

This completeness is, of course, known as waking up, receiving the knowledge or enlightenment and, to people on the spiritual pathway, the pinnacle of life. Actually, it is just an experience that one can never forget, but life continues as before with all the ups and downs that one is used to.

The experience, however, changes one's perception of relation-ships with people and the environment, because this *knowing* will always be felt as the Oneness is translated into love. Therefore, while life continues as before with regard to day-to-day necessities, the personality and need to serve one's fellow man becomes uppermost in life. This service is then a way of life and, through this attachment to all life, takes on a meaning not known previously.

This awakening is open to all, the biggest obstacle being one's lack of confidence and lack of love for oneself. By relaxing into one's inner self, it brings a closeness to God or All That Is and with it the love permeating through every cell, which bursts forth in an outward show of happiness and care for all life.

Happiness

Happiness is the Utopia for most people as it is usually only experienced fleetingly. No sooner does it arrive than it disappears again. How, then, can happiness become permanent? It is down to many things, not least one's attitude to all people and beings around you as you go through your day. You can start off with all good intentions and then be affected by the first problem that confronts you. Others may start off their day in a negative manner and their day can be improved by someone or some positive experience that brings happiness for a while.

So, it appears that in most cases people's happiness is affected by outside influences, but the reverse can happen when operating from inside influences. By starting the day from within, being in contact with your spiritual side, soul, higher self, God aspect, or whatever you wish to call it, then your whole demeanour changes to one of equilibrium, appearing to others as calm and peaceful. You can then avoid the continuous highs and lows, which are normal in most people's lives, whether the period between them be short or long.

Many look for happiness through drink or drugs, or both, and for a time they seem to work, but when the effects wear off the negative periods seem longer and so it can become a vicious circle, where more and more drink or drugs are needed to achieve the state they are looking for. There are many ways people search for happiness and, when achieved, they try to hold on to it and wonder why they fail. It is because there is a natural flow of highs and lows in life and by trying to change them by outward means has the effect of accentuating these periods, with lows gradually becoming more prevalent.

We are all given the necessary tools at birth to live life to the full, without the need to resort to unnatural aids as these eventually defeat the object of finding permanent happiness.

The only guaranteed way of finding happiness is from within

where a peaceful contentment is felt and can be carried into daily life. An urge to help other people usually follows and, when this call is taken up in whatever form is appropriate, then the act of helping or serving others inevitably results in happiness within and without. It is a natural occurrence that just appears without trying and recurs again and again, following a change in one's priorities and outlook, until contentment or happiness beyond expectations is felt on a more permanent basis.

Therefore, replacing selfishness with a love for others, translated into service, is a real antidote for unhappiness.

Endurance

It is by enduring hardships that the soul experiences that which is necessary for its growth. You all have difficulties in your lives for that is the way it is meant to be. These difficulties are in your plan for this lifetime, so please don't reject them or wish they were not happening. We know it is natural for you to feel this, but afterwards you feel pleased they are over and sometimes you wonder how you got through them. In fact you occasionally wonder if the Divine hand had a part to play. You would probably be right, but not always, of course.

If your lives were like a bed of roses all the time you may enjoy that way of life for a short time but inside you would want something else also. You all like variation in life as nobody wants to be stagnant. So, with the change it is inevitable that problems will arise. It is not so much the result that counts but rather the way you handle these situations.

Think of it like this: if everything in your life was always cosy with nothing unusual happening, how would your soul grow? It is in the problems that it does grow. It may be hard for you to realise but before you began this sojourn on earth you agreed to various different scenarios - rather like a blueprint but still leaving room for many manoeuvres within it - because if everything was pre-planned what would be the point of it all? It is rather like being in different mazes, some easy and others difficult. Once your own maze had been selected you would have the choice of many different avenues to go down before finding the ultimate one, when you realise your life is now on course. Then you are ready for the next challenge, which may be a harder maze, and so on.

Your soul is aware of this, if you are not, but you all have felt at times that you have been in a particular situation before. Sometimes it is to give you another go at it, and at other times it is to give you a little respite.

Many people question the purpose of this life and are unable to comprehend that it is a continuous journey of the soul on the road back to God. It appears, when you are on earth, that you only have one life and, as such, there does not seem to be any real purpose behind it, especially if one has no faith or spiritual understanding. There is a reason you don't remember previous lives or, indeed, your time in spirit, for if you were aware of this it would have a dramatic effect on this life. Suffice it to say, knowing that this is not your only life can make a big difference. When you return to spirit, after this life, you will then be given sufficient information, as necessary, about previous lives to make sense of this one. Even if you were then given all your life stories you would not be able to assimilate all the information at once. Indeed, there may be a lot you would not want to hear and you could also find it hard to take details at the other extreme.

When we talk about *you* we are not referring to one body that reincarnates over and over again, because it is not like that. It would seem that one soul would have a new body each time it reincarnated, but this soul might be part of a bigger group of souls. We can see from here more of the overall picture and, as evolution is happening all the time, part of a particular group may contain young and old souls. After undergoing certain life patterns the knowledge and experiences gained can be pooled for the benefit of all.

As previously explained it is not simple and now is not the time to go further into it. However, with this little knowledge we hope and trust that the endurance you sometimes feel in this lifetime will be more than worthwhile when taken as a whole, and as you look back on it after completing your successful earth sojourn.

Changing Vibrations

You keep a diary to organise and manage your time; so, who keeps the diary to ensure the solar system, galaxies and universe work to exact timings? Without a mastermind you would not be able to live in your bodies as there would be no air or food to sustain them. As your scientists and mathematicians study the heavens more astounding evidence is seen; how the precision of the orbital patterns of the planets around the sun, as well as stars and galaxies orbiting their larger parental ones, is constantly taking place so that there is exact order in the universe.

God, that super-intelligence, ensures the physical universe lives and evolves to His Divine Order. The more the universe is investigated the more incredible it seems, as it is apparently ever-expanding and renewed as old stars die and new ones are born. What could possibly be behind this miracle if not some super-mind we call God? No wonder the early humans worshipped the sun and solar system, as their young minds could see the Divine in the heavenly bodies.

Modern man may have all scientific inventions that make the world seem smaller than it really is, but he or she still cannot understand the God behind all life. In fact, many do not even believe in God and think the universe and everyone and everything within it works randomly without any Divine guidance and inspiration.

What should we think of modern discoveries today? Are they following a pattern of randomness or are they all part of the Divine plan? We say to you that the Divine is at work, allowing these discoveries as His plan evolves and as more people are drawn to a feeling of preparedness for the New Age. As the higher vibrations take place on earth so your bodies will notice a difference as the spiritual aspect becomes more prominent. People will not suddenly be lifted into space, or the astral regions, but they will experience an upliftment in their minds and nervous systems, as their body as a whole reacts to the higher vibrations. This upliftment will affect their Oneness with nature and All That Is and may make them light-headed at times. This is nothing to fear and, as the changes are made, the body will adjust to its higher vibrations through its own spirit and mind.

The effects on people will differ according to their understanding and life plans. However, initially, some of the world's population, who know not what is happening, will face fear and hardship and even more conflicts throughout the world will occur while these adjustments are felt. Gradually they will be translated into changing philosophies across the globe and, in the transition period, which will not be easy, people will be assisted as the spiritual way of life is adopted by more and more of the population.

These changes are happening now, with some feeling them already, as they are prepared, with help from us, to spread the age-old wisdom in a manner that can be understood by all. Those of you who are ready will soon know what is expected of you, so that you play your part in the teaching and explanation of these spiritual values, as you become the forerunners or harbingers of the new Golden Age.

Crossroads

You may be at a crossroads in your life, feeling there is something more to it, that you could be doing something else, or you may even feel insecure. How many have experienced this? It is quite normal when you have led busy lives that you feel something is missing. It is then that you are ready to question the real meaning of life and what would make you more fulfilled.

It is probably your soul prompting you to explore and look for more, within and without yourself, and to push you to look for knowledge that you hadn't considered up to that point in your life. So stop, pause, and take a good look at yourself. Your life may be exciting, habitual or humdrum but something is tugging away at you to find what is missing. It is not out there, my friends, for what you are looking for is within you. This may sound strange if you have, up to this point in time, been looking outside for new interests and knowledge.

Where do you think ideas and inspirations come from? That's right, it is from within, usually after you have slept or been quiet for a while. You may suddenly realise you know what to do in a given situation that has been concerning you, or you receive that last piece in the jigsaw, so to speak, to enable you to move forward in some way. Everything, all knowledge and answers are potentially within oneself, in that God centre which can be found in the silence when one is ready for a spiritual awakening. Most people have been asleep to that side of life and it is ready and waiting for you to make the first move. You may have been prompted or thought about it many times but until you are ready to surrender to the unknown within you will not receive what you have been waiting for.

Once you make that first move you will receive a bountiful response from your real or higher self. You will feel guided in all sorts of ways which will lead you to feelings of love, peace and joy and, although you may not understand what is happening, there will always be help on the way from seen and unseen friends. People will appear in your life, sometimes for a short period and others for much longer, to answer your questions and probably lead you in new directions. Books and new knowledge may suddenly appear and you will have a longing for more as you continue your quest for the spiritual side of life.

At the same time you will have a completely new outlook where you will love all life, and a way of helping your fellow man will somehow appear before you when you are ready. You will not be alone on this journey, although it may appear so, as old friends may not understand your new way of life and ideals and drop out of your life. However, you will be helped from within and new friends and acquaintances will fill the gap.

You will be taken down new avenues, with often unexpected results, and you will experience untold joys, love, peace and that fulfilment you had been longing for but had never expected to find.

Universal Power

We greet you today from the realms of spirit and bring love, peace and truth in words for your consideration. We have gone a little way further down the road than you on earth and can see the overall picture of your situations, rather than just a one-sided view which you experience.

We are not talking about anyone being more advanced than another because we are all One under the Great Divine Mind. We are all connected and at the very centre of everyone is the power which emits and receives as one goes through life. You would call it 'giving and taking' although people are not generally conscious of this spiritual truth. This universal power is like a golden light that stretches forth from the Infinite, in and through all life, to the edges of the universe although, of course, there are no edges to the universe because in essence it is an enormous circle, almost oval in shape, ever-pulsating with energy.

You are able to tap into this universal energy because the power of love within the universe and everyone is the same, the only difference being in the degree, or level, within all spirit and physical matter. At the heart of matter is this spiritual essence and explains why you and we are at One with all life.

How do you think we are able to communicate between the two worlds? It is because we link in to this Divine connection within us all. Very few of you feel this connection permanently, but many who come close to it have wonderful experiences within and in their relationship with all life. You can tap into it in your meditation and it can grow into a regular occurrence with a humble outpouring of love, as prayer, in your daily life.

The great Masters have and are able to perform miracles as they are permanently at One with this intangible power of love. They can change the structure of matter, whether it is an object or something in nature. In fact nothing is impossible for these great ones, some of whom are still at work on earth, whether or not you see them, as they are able to step between the two worlds at will. They may not appear to be in the form in which the world knew them but they are there, nevertheless, as the preparations continue in the changing vibrations of the earth.

Therefore, my friends, nothing is impossible and as you feel a closer affinity to All That Is in your meditations, or indeed at any time, you will be coming into the great truth that all is One. This is felt in your hearts and as more and more of you have this experience then you will be playing your part in bringing the Divine plan of spiritually transforming your planet into being.

Cause and Effect

'You come into this world with nothing and you leave with nothing' is a common quote and refers to the physical assets acquired during a lifetime. What are far more important are the spiritual riches that are gained. These you do take with you into your next life, along with your karma. People commonly only think of so-called bad karma but good karma is equally important and displays the soul's evolving progress.

The natural law of cause and effect cannot be avoided, but can be mitigated by the intention of the actions involved. There is naturally a balance to take forward into your next life. You have all met people who spend their whole life helping others and are known as the person to call upon when one is in trouble. This sort of person is creating a wonderful abode in his or her next life, whereas at the other end of the scale there may be a scrounger who only thinks of his or her self and expects everything to be done for them.

Karma is, therefore, a great leveller in times to come and should never be underestimated. It affects the whole of one's life, from relationships at home, at work and in recreation. One's thoughts lead to actions so the saying 'think before you act' has never been so important in relation to karma.

There are no little men spying on you, giving out good and bad marks, during your life. Rather, actions are automatically recorded in your soul, and in everyone's soul, through the interconnectedness of all life. You are your own severest critic, when reviewing your life, after passing over to the other side. You will relive every detail, which can be uplifting, demoralising or somewhere in-between. Most lives will have a balance, but all will feel the need to correct any wrongs done on earth. You are the one judging your own life, not some parental or other higher figure close to you. It is personal and although there are so-called Lords of Karma they are only there to help and advise, not to judge or criticise in any way.

Sai Baba said 'Hands that help are holier than lips that pray' and this is so relevant in relation to karma. A life of devotion to the Lord, without actions of service to one's fellow man, is nothing compared to a life of devotion accompanied by service to mankind. This love in action is godly and builds up treasures in heaven.

Although some people seem to be born into a happy life of service they have actually worked for it over a long period, sometimes lifetimes. Therefore, when some bemoan their misfortunes, especially if they are bored or depressed, then there is no greater healing than for them to think about and help others. They will then not have time to think of themselves and, through loving and serving others, they will consequently transform their own lives.

As you contemplate your life make time to sit silently and follow the still small voice within to guide you forward into a life of loving action.

Closeness to God

'God be with you' is a wonderful greeting whether taken literally or not. You may know that God is within everyone and everything, even in the tiniest cell of the body. Why then don't people act accordingly in their everyday lives? You can't stop your God going with you because there is never a time that He is *not* with you. People who are aware that God is within seem to need reminding regularly, otherwise they get so involved in the day's events that they tend to forget.

Remind yourselves then, in any way that helps you to remember whether it is by mantra, prayer or recognising a feeling of love or warmth within. For God is at the heart of everyone and everything you encounter in your daily activities. As you become proficient at reminding yourselves then you will automatically dedicate all your thoughts and actions to the Lord, for they are His in the first place. Living this way, constantly reminding yourselves of this great wisdom, will lead you to dedicate your whole life to God, with unbelievable results.

Without realising it you are literally handing over your life, the very personal you, to your God and a strange thing often happens. Your ego will take a back seat as the *old* you gradually disappears and the *new* you takes over your life. You will appear to be directed from within as the future pathway becomes wider and easier to follow, leading to a growing in confidence which, in turn, is followed by peace and joy in all aspects of your life.

It is not as though you are doing anything substantially different but it is actually in the manner you do things and your attitude of mind that are behind this change.

You become subconsciously aware of the interaction with your Divine essence at all times, resulting in happiness beyond description. To others you will appear to have a guiding light shining forth, together with magnetism, and people will want a share in this attraction of unconditional love.

The Book of Life

Life is an opportunity to experience all those things in the physical that cannot be felt anywhere else in the universe. A life spent on earth should be cherished and allows one to taste that which is not available in spirit. Your bodies are so much heavier to meet the needs of the physical and many people seem to live in difficult circumstances wherever they are in the world. This has often been brought about by the way they treated their bodies earlier in life, also through old age and, of course, having agreed to these challenges pre-birth.

You are born to the appropriate parents and in the right location for your soul's growth. You quickly adapt to your new surroundings and so begin your new life with the memory of all previous lives and experiences having been removed, so that you gain the maximum out of this sojourn on earth. You may be born to rich, poor or in-between families, or even as an orphan, but all have the same opportunities for soul growth through the many different journeys that life takes you on.

The body has many highs and lows on its journey but, to its advantage, it can feel and touch other people, animals or material objects. The senses enable it to cement relationships in a glorious way for the procreation of the human race.

It is, however, a privilege to earn a human life but many people, being unaware of this, abuse their bodies in various ways, thus bringing upon themselves unexpected problems in health, both mental and physical. So, my friends, look upon your life as a Divine gift and treasure it with all the opportunities given and be eternally grateful to your Father in heaven. By regularly reminding yourselves that God is the Provider will change your attitude and this positive outlook encourages the cells of the body to be healthy which, in turn, assists in an improvement in vitality and health, if necessary.

As one explores the highways and byways of this life the soul will attract people and relationships to it, to promote growth. Some may be easy and free-flowing while others may be difficult and sometimes outrageously unbearable. They may be of short duration or long-lasting but all, without doubt, will bring necessary learning on both sides. When looking back with an open mind on these activities one can see where the learning has, in fact, occurred.

All have within them the desire to improve, explore and expand their lives by finding new or variations on existing activities and in this you will, without realising it, be guided in the right direction. Whether you follow this guidance is entirely up to you as you have your own free will. As with the other sections, or chapters, of your life this will determine whether the individual follows his or her chosen pathway and either completes the anticipated soul development or languishes behind, having been drawn into intense material experiences, rather than creating a balance between the spiritual and physical life.

A person can be highly spiritual without the airs and graces or outward appearances of being a religious follower or, indeed, searching for hidden treasures within. It is people's thoughts and actions for others, human or animal, that also determine the spiritual progress of the soul. The demonstration of worshipping as a habit or show, rather than in sincerity, counts for nothing unless it is accompanied by a genuine love for God through service to mankind.

These are unique times in the history of the earth and, as the New Age approaches, there will be many openings for people to take on the mantle of harbingers as the *real* truths are brought to the population. Then more and more will have an urge within to explore and learn the teachings of the Masters. These teachings will be given in modern terminology, through different channels and communication, as appropriate, to the cultures and modern thinking of the people. The anticipated change in vibrations on the earth will speed up this transition period, as people will answer the call within to not only search for the truth, but many will themselves become teachers of this wisdom with a demonstration of a new way of life. It will display a care and love for not only your families and immediate neighbour, but also through feeling that unconditional love inspiring one to help and serve all mankind.

This precious life on earth, with all its different chapters, will be appreciated for what it is, a unique gift from God to experience and savour the wonders of the earth with the purity of air, water and nature returning through the dedication of the people, creating a balance of material and spiritual values once more.

Moribund or Carefree

Life can be moribund or carefree. From time immemorial man has been chasing that elusive freedom of mind and soul. Now is the time to look inwards for that goal, that everlasting love, that peace which is available to all. It only requires strength of purpose and resolve to pursue the apparent lost dream.

How, then, in the ever-increasing noise and interference of the natural flow of nature and energy, can man return to the simple way of life? Firstly, he or she needs to take time to be with himself or herself in the quiet of the heart. By making time for this each day it creates a centring of mind, body and soul, a foundation of balance that can stay with one for the whole day.

Now, my friends, to restore nature to its natural rhythm it starts with you. Instead of making every aspect of life faster let go, and in so doing you will find that life that sped at 100 mph yesterday will change and you will begin to experience its beautiful intricacies. The look of joy and amazement on a child's face, the beautiful smile of someone at peace, the faithful look and composure of a dog awaiting its master's instructions: the beauty of wild and cultivated flowers, of lovingly tended gardens, and the sheer magnificence of a raging sea against the background of a ragged rocky coastline. All these are small examples of life that can be appreciated or ignored, depending upon one's attitude to life and environment.

The bleakest landscape or poorest neighbourhood can be transformed inwardly, as your images of the same scene will vary according to your state of mind. From the enthusiastic person who sees within the outer impression and finds the reality of God in all life, to the downtrodden person who sees everything distorted and grey where life is a drudge, there is within all the potential to see the truth that nothing is actually as it appears on the surface.

Now, how to explain this is not easy but all the make-up of

living beings and inanimate objects is continually moving. Bodies and furniture, for example, are not solid as they appear to you. The neutrons, protons and electrons within the atom are revolving around the nucleus. Likewise the molecules and cells within the whole body are moving in the Divine energy, which is connected to all other beings and life. Hence, there is only the One to which all are invisibly attached, so you are all like limbs of the One Body. It seems to everyone that they are individuals, as it feels this way, and this is actually the big illusion of life.

It is quite normal to feel that you are an individual and, indeed, you would find life almost impossible on earth if that were not how it seemed. The truth is, nevertheless, that we are all One and you can sometimes feel you are connected to all life in meditation, or when you are engrossed in music, the arts, beauty of the world or, in fact, anything that takes your attention away from normal activities that remind you of your assumed individual status.

How can you make use of the profound truth that all is One under the Divine umbrella? To those hearing this truth for the first time it can be overwhelming with a mixture of incredulousness and worry that you may lose your individualism, or ego. In fact, life carries on as normal, wood still needs to be chopped, washing and cooking still need to be done and there is no real outward change.

The change, of course, is within and affects your total outlook, for if we are all One, why argue, or get one up on your neighbour, or act selfishly to the detriment of a fellow part of the Godhead? Yes, it can create a radical change in one's thoughts, behaviour and in one's values and relationship with everyone and everything. This could lead to Utopia, through a life seen as an outpouring of unconditional love, peace, truth, right action and non-violence, which has formed the basis of the teachings of the great Masters down the ages.

So, why don't we see it happening regularly today, as there are many who have heard these teachings and believed them? That is, of course, the big question. Hearing the truth and living it only go together when one is ready, when the mind, body and soul come together in harmony. How many times do you see people going to retreats, away from normal life, appearing to be ready, only for the resolve to disappear within a few days of returning home.

Conditions are changing, my friends. The earth's vibrations are increasing and the time is fast approaching when more and more of you will hear the ancient wisdom and know within that it is time to join the growing band of pilgrims; to be examples to the rest of the population as you become at One with all life. Your devotion to the Almighty will show you as a being of love and light, putting into practice your values by demonstrating a new way of life in service to your fellow man.

The balance of mind, body and spirit will show forth as you go about your daily tasks with a lightness and inner glow, transforming your demeanour, confidence and energy for all to see. Many will be influenced as they come in contact with you and will then need to look at their own lives anew. A growing number of teachers will become ready to satisfy the needs of the people as the Divine plan comes to fruition and the Golden Age will at last be dawning upon the earth in all its glory.

More to Life and Death

When you send condolences to relations and friends of someone who has passed to this side of life we celebrate the return of a soul who has completed his or her sojourn on earth. We know this is hard for most people to understand but a life on earth is only for a short time in relation to the eternity we all have. A friend returning to us would be like someone coming back to you from an expedition or other lengthy trip. It sometimes takes a little while to readjust to life here, especially if the transition had been sudden, but he or she is given all the love and care necessary to complete the journey.

For some little or no adjustment is necessary as they already have sufficient knowledge, having probably lived a life of service on earth and been in tune with their real selves. Your future abode here is built from your current life and previous incarnations, and it will feel quite natural when you settle into your new home. The ideas of heaven and hell may seem way off the mark to people who have some knowledge of life after death, but, to a degree, they make sense in that you build up riches or rags in your next life by the way you live your present one.

Some may be so materialistic and tied to the earth that a few souls do not make the transition in the normal way. They are moribund and literally stuck to the earth, lost, not knowing where they are or what is happening. We are, therefore, indebted to those of you who run rescue circles and thus help these lost souls find their way here into the light.

You bring with you on each incarnation sufficient past experiences to sustain your time on earth. Even though you don't remember previous lives you have an in-built knowing, courage and fortitude to help you through difficult times, and all of you can tap into this storehouse as you traverse life's pathways and meet the challenges you encounter. You all have equal opportunities on earth to make progress on your journey back to the Godhead. It may appear, by earthly standards, that there are so many inequalities in your lives but each of you has precisely the conditions and circumstances necessary to fulfil the goals set by you before you were born.

To see what can be achieved look at the gentleness of someone in tune with the universe. It is a blessing for anyone in the vicinity of this great soul, for the attraction is there for all to see and feel. Nothing is rushed, as the calmness precedes everything being done, and each one present is caught up in the magnet or aura of this being. All actions seem to be carried out without effort, with no thought given to time as it works out to the exact minute. This state can be reached when one lets go of the individual and becomes the whole in thought, word and deed, having handed over completely to All That Is.

Living your life from within is the only sure way as your real self resides there. So, start the day in this way and feel the love in your heart centre; then link in during the day and, as this becomes a habit, you will find that you are sometimes at One on a certain level. This way of life is open to everyone wherever they are and whatever they are doing. All it takes is a desire to become close to your God with a strong resolve and commitment to follow the dictates of your heart, the still small voice within, sometimes called your conscience, which really is your higher self, or God, talking to you.

It may not be easy at first to distinguish this premier thought from all the other everyday ones rushing in and out of your mind, but in time you will begin to recognise the difference. The real voice within will usually be accompanied by a loving, peaceful, warm feeling. However, during the hustle and bustle of your busy days you may not have time to await this feeling, but by then, with experience, you will be able to rely on this special voice. As it grows stronger your inner sense becomes a knowing and the experience of being at One, only temporarily at first will, nevertheless, be in the background as you go through life. The ups and downs will seem less intense as a feeling of equanimity pervades your body, mind and soul.

You will finally be completely at One and experience your heaven while still on earth.

Part Four

Getting to Know Oneself

Infinite Life

As we come together today we think of those dear friends who were so close to us over the years. There is no death as life is infinite; you are born into a life on earth, which may vary in length widely, but you can be sure that this earthly life is only for a short period in your eternal life.

We know that for you on earth it appears to be your only life until, or unless, you have a belief, or knowing, that the soul or spirit never dies. How could it die, my friends, when it is part of the eternal Spirit of All?

So, when you have this knowing that there is no death then the passing of a friend, or member of family, to this side of life is tempered by that knowledge. You miss the human frame, personality, the love between you, and this can be difficult after many years together. Nevertheless, you will know that when it is your turn to traverse the great divide, you will be met by your loved ones and such a greeting it will be, for we, here, celebrate your return. We are conscious of those left behind and, as feelings are so intense here we, too, miss you who are still on the earth.

So, today, may you rejoice in the knowledge that there is no death and that you may enjoy life to the full, knowing that when it is your turn to join us you will have experienced a life full of joy and happiness mixed, naturally, with some unhappiness and difficulties, but in the knowledge that nothing can ever harm the spirit within.

We celebrate with you the lives of those who have passed to the higher world, as it is sometimes known, and we comfort those on your side who are grieving for the loss of their loved ones, and especially those who do not believe in an afterlife.

We are, therefore, with those of you today and forever who need our love at difficult times in their lives, but especially for those who are grieving at this time. May they know or come to know that all life is eternal.

Foundations

There is a foundation for everything. Nature has a foundation and all life, as we know it, has a foundation. Your individual lives are based on the foundation within. Most people say their lives are based on their conditioning and their surroundings. This does have an effect on them but it is their soul and spirit that determines their foundation for this life. Each soul contains all experiences of previous lives, so, when coming to the earth you bring with you your history, your combination of all lives, resulting in who you have now become. You are equipped with the necessary gifts to live this current life according to your life plan.

This is where the so-called conditioning, parents and early contacts, come in to mould certain personality traits for you, but your inner soul reflects your basic character, which you have built from previous lives. It, of course, seems to you that this is your only life as all previous ones have been wiped from your memory.

Nevertheless, you all have some inclinations and leanings in certain areas, with clues sometimes evident of your previous existences. In the main, however, it is as though it is your only life and many, many, think that is, indeed, the truth. Many more also do not believe in an afterlife, so it takes a long time for them to become accustomed to life in the spirit world when they cast off their human bodies. Those who have a knowing that there is no death find the crossing very smooth and a natural part of existence. All are welcomed upon arrival by their loved ones and help is at hand, where necessary, for all those in shock and disbelief that there is a future life.

The ones who have prepared themselves, knowing within that there is no death, will settle into their new way of life quickly. For them it will simply be like stepping from one room to another. Therefore, when you have an opportunity to investigate and come to understand about life after so-called death you will have a greater advantage when your turn comes to cross the divide and your knowledge of and faith in God will also ease the transition to your new life.

So, my friends, enjoy this life, experience it to the full and come to know that there is so much more to life than appears on the surface.

Heaven or Hell

There is a place for everyone in the afterlife, whoever they are, from king to pauper. From saint to murderer there is a place, for you are all part of the Great Spirit and, as such, your consciousness never dies.

Yes, you leave behind your body and all your material goods. You cannot take anything with you other than your inner real self which contains your soul and spirit. You also leave behind your family, friends and acquaintances. As they mourn for you, you will come into the most glorious light you have ever seen and will be welcomed by those who have gone ahead of you on this journey.

You will be shown your new home, which you have made for yourself out of the life you have led on the earth. Your thoughts and actions, but above all your love for your fellow beings, will create your new home. For those who, for one reason or another, have not shown a loving or caring attitude on earth, and may have done the reverse of service in life, their new homes will be denser and darker.

On the other hand, those of you who have served your brothers and sisters with unconditional love, and care for all life will find their homes bright, full of joy and beauty beyond belief.

You are all on your own pathways and these, too, have a bearing on your new life in spirit. You, therefore, earn your new homes with us when it is time for you to make the crossing from your side of life.

Heaven and hell are actually within you during your sojourn on earth and you have all experienced degrees of heaven and hell at times. You, therefore, take with you this state of being into the next life and it is manifested when you arrive here with us. Many of you will need to rest a while before getting used to your new circumstances.

Others, who are full of joy and understanding when they cross over, will have a most beautiful experience during their crossing and will immediately adjust to their new way of life.

So, when you are sitting and thinking about your life on earth spare a thought for the abode and conditions you are building for your next life in spirit.

A Hint of Spirit Life

We come to you today full of life, full of energy and full of light, for we are like light to each other. We can show our bodies but we instinctively know each other through feeling and thought. Yes, we too have minds; it is a thought world where we live and the beauty is beyond imagination.

Your world, to you, is so beautiful, especially when seen from space: that superb blue globe with the green of the forests, the rain forests teeming with life, your golden beaches, beautiful rivers and incredibly large oceans.

This is nothing, my friends, compared with our world. When I say our world I mean our environment. We have such strong and delicate colours with superb gardens and landscapes. The sun is always out but it is not hot. We don't need rest or sleep, like you do, for we are permanently awake.

There are many different areas of life, each appropriate to the soul residing here. Without saying too much we can say that we are aware of the different levels and we are visited often by the higher beings, which you would know as Masters and Archangels. We, too, have celebrations with music, so peaceful yet invigorating, with vibrant colours emitting from the sound and blending with the surroundings.

We receive wonderful discourses from these higher beings who, to us, appear pure white, pure light. At the other end of the scale we visit other realms, not as fortunate as us, where the conditions become denser. We, in turn, are able to talk and assist them in their realms whereas, when in our natural home, we work and build by thought. We learn and teach. We have a full range of the arts and there is never a dull moment, as you would describe it, and many of us are engrossed in the work of bringing the teachings to people on earth through channels like you. As we speak we can see other groups coming together receiving the teachings and being prepared for the work ahead.

My friends, we can see you as you really are, bundles of light and love and beauty. You will one day see yourselves this way and the peace you will feel is beyond description. We will leave you now in this well of light, love and peace.

Relationships

Today we would like to talk about relationships; relationships to one another, to the animal kingdom, to the earth, but above all to the One Great Mind, God. Most people are not aware of the interconnectedness of all beings. Therefore, to talk about relationship with those people will have a different meaning from talking about it with those who have some spiritual understanding.

For many in the first category competition is a major factor in their lives, which often leads to them wanting more than the people around them. This sometimes creates jealousy and one-upmanship and is totally different from the relationship we are talking about, where lives are based upon the foundation of God at the heart of everything.

Most people think about relationships between men and women in love, marriage for example, or these days partnerships, where they fall in love, set up home together and raise a family. Relationship is then not just about the union of husband and wife but also about the one with their children and vice versa.

Relationships are ongoing and may be work or leisure-related but, in fact, they are made every time you meet someone, even as you pass them on the street with a nod, a smile or complete ignorance; it is still a relationship, whether for a brief second or much longer. They come in all manner of situations from neighbours, social, shopping expeditions, to all types of meetings, and in your lifetimes you make a myriad of them. From the shortest to the longest relationship all have one thing in common, the meeting of one form of God to another.

We are always hearing your disparaging remarks about people or, alternatively, your complimentary remarks. How, then, would people react if they realised they were talking to a son or daughter of God? There would be a radical change in the basis of all relationships. We realise that all people are unique and have such differing personalities and it is quite normal that one cannot get on with everyone because of the way that some people act. However, if you have the belief, the knowing that God is within all, then you are able to afford them the respect and love that then comes naturally. But, even when people do have this knowledge, we still hear criticisms and judgements, people falling out with one another and apparently forgetting who they really are.

It is not easy to always remember who you are, but spending time within can change all your attitudes in relation to one another and all life. Would some people still be cruel to animals, or treat the earth and its resources in such a flippant way if they had this knowledge? No, my friends, relationships start with the most important one, the one with your God. We are not just talking about rituals but your relationship within, which can, indeed, be by communication and when it reaches an intense feeling of love then words may not be necessary. As you forge your relationship with God so all your other ones will be affected and, in time, be based on the unconditional love you can feel within. Your relationship with all life then changes and blossoms as your whole manner and attitude to all people and beings becomes one of love, where you see the best in everyone rather than their petty deficiencies.

My friends, this is a difficult subject to discuss for, as the saying goes, you are only human and sometimes it seems to give people the excuse to behave badly to each other. We would say to you then that you are, indeed, human but, more than that, you were created in the image of, and by, God and, as such, to therefore live a life reflecting the knowledge that you now have.

Angelic Forces

We come to you today in peace and love to talk about the work of the angelic forces on earth. Many of you think the talk of angels is just a fairy tale while others of you, a minority, have actually seen the nature spirits.

We are here to tell you that they do, indeed, exist and can be seen by those with eyes to see them. They can be found in gardens, in fields and they are certainly not in one's imagination. They are there to help nature perform its duty, and at this time of pollution on your earth they perform even more important tasks. They are happy and peaceful as they go about their work. They do not have free will, but have love in their hearts and thrive on their complete devotion to All That Is. They are very close to the human race but do not interfere in any way as you all have your own lives to lead.

We will now talk a little about guardian angels. These are, in fact, guides and you all have one that is with you throughout your earthly life. Again, the guardian angel does not interfere with your free will, but helps to create the conditions for you to experience your pathway in this life. Other guides come to you at certain stages of your life, especially as you progress on the inner spiritual levels. Most people are not aware of their angels or guides, and you, who are aware, are privileged to know you have them all around you. You can call on them at any time just by thinking of them. They will know what is required and, for those who work to increase the spiritual knowledge on earth, they are there to inspire you and others when called upon and will assist you to fulfil your life plan.

You would have known your guides before this incarnation and they are only too happy to serve you, and the public, as you help to bring the age-old wisdoms and philosophies to your earth at this time. So, welcome them, interact with them, feel them with you, for you will be working together for some time and they have prepared themselves over a very long period to fulfil their obligations to you. We say obligations but they don't feel it as an obligation at all as they have love in their hearts, a willingness to serve you and all people and, of course, they are fulfilling their particular aspect of the Divine plan.

When you sit in meditation you can feel them with you as this is when they are able to be close and communicate with you; this becomes stronger as you naturally open up to them.

We stress again that you all have free will. Nothing is inflicted upon you on the way, but you will have an inner motivation to work with us when the time is right for you. You have known your guides over many lifetimes and it is a real pleasure for them to work with you. We know this seems rather strange to many of you but they bring such love and peace to provide the correct conditions to help you fulfil your life plan.

So, we say to you, open up your channels with love and devotion to be of service to mankind as we prepare, on our part, the stage in readiness for your work.

At the Start of the Day

As you enter into the start of yet another day on earth we bring to you love and blessings from spirit. In fact, we don't really bring them to you because they are within, around, above and below, always. However, by saying we bring them allows you to focus on your real self, that part of you that is all light and love and is inherently within every cell. You may feel it in your heart centre but, one day, you will feel it permeating throughout you and through the universe.

What a statement, my friends, for it means there is no place you can go, within, and anywhere in your world, where this love is not active. It may appear to be still but it is pulsating at the heart of every living being. For those of you who are aware of this truth it enables you to rest in that sacred place within and become replenished, re-energised and full of confidence, knowing that you are not really alone at any time.

As you enter a new day not only are your bodies recharged after sleep, but feeling the love within gives you additional fortitude and courage to face whatever experiences or problems that may occur in your lives today. It enables one to be transformed from a pessimist to an optimist, with a keen anticipation for the life ahead.

Loneliness is a sad reflection of society in your world today in the way that people can be on their own, physically, for some considerable time in certain cases. Others, although appearing to be with other people, nevertheless seem to be lonely. The reality is that no one needs to be alone when they are aware of the truth that the Lord God is within all people and all beings. Therefore, by connecting to the Great Spirit it means that one will never be alone again, whether that loneliness is physical or due to lack of confidence when being with other people.

So, my friends, it can be a happy day for you when you put this knowledge into practice and feel the love within. It is always with you and waiting to be passed on to others in need, whether that need is physical, mental or spiritual. A casual touch, a smile, encouragement or physically helping in some way or another is distributing in your world the wonderful positive energy of universal love.

Take time then, at the start of each day, to be with your real self, knowing that in partnership with the Holy Spirit you can achieve greatness and have a real purpose as you bring light and happiness to your fellow pilgrims on the way to becoming at One with All That Is.

All That Is

All That Is. What does that conjure up in your minds? The whole world, everything in it, everything seen or unseen, the whole universe, all life? It is such a broad statement, so powerful, that the real meaning can easily be missed.

All That Is. Surely, everything, everyone is included. The human mind cannot comprehend it, especially when looking at all the stars on a clear night, for example.

All That Is. If you asked a hundred people what it meant you would probably receive a hundred different answers! We would like to say that it does, indeed, incorporate all life here, all life on your earth and beyond; but also, and more importantly, it includes the thought that God is experiencing life in the physical and spiritual spheres.

The spiritual spheres, my friends, are not just in the world of spirit but are, in fact, also within your very selves. You can be in contact with the spiritual sphere within and, in so doing, you are potentially in contact with all life. How does that make you feel?

To people who understand it is a most wonderful revelation for, although you haven't learnt how to do so yet, you could be in touch with the furthest star, the new born baby, a friend on the other side of the world, or with any life anywhere, even within the rain forests.

How can this possibly be? we hear you say. It is because the Great Spirit is within every atom and that all atoms throughout the universe are in contact with one another through the space therein, leading to the interconnectedness of all life. You don't have to go within the atom, of course, just simply be still and quiet within and you will eventually receive revelation upon revelation as you enter and stay in that incredible world.

All friendships are made from within, and all inventions are from within. It may not appear so but that is where new ideas and new frontiers emerge. So, rest in that peace whenever you can. You will find something extraordinary happening in your lives as new vistas are opened up and you find yourselves expanding, both spiritually and materially, as life takes on new channels for you to explore.

Remember, my friends, it is the Great One that is within all life and may rightly be called All That Is

Moment to Moment

We bring to you love and peace as you begin another day on your earth. Do you feel and hear the silence all around you? It is tangible for all things from God are tangible, even if they are not seen, as it is in the unseen that creating is forged. Rest and dwell in this beautiful silence for a little while as you are enveloped in the elegance and strength of this moment. You can feel lost in these conditions as you feel at One with All That Is

Take time to appreciate this gift where you feel all life surrounding you. For it is in times like this that you are recharged and receive the peace and love to sustain you as you enter upon the stage of living. True living, my friends, is being aware of the moment and all that it contains, for it actually contains everything.

You are then at peace with yourselves and your surroundings and it is incomparable with the normal experience of one's day. It, the moment, contains healing rays that go through the body into all the cells where they are invigorated. It is even better for you than sleep, so take this glorious feeling within you, in the moment. Take it with you as your day unfolds and you will be inspired in all you plan and do.

The day can be full or empty. It makes no difference if you take this love and peace throughout it. You will be given light and understanding as you wonder what is ahead of you all. Instead of rushing headlong through your day, take time to appreciate the finer moments of your experiences. You all say that time is going faster than you can ever remember. So, why is this? It is because you are trying to fit so many things into your day rather than letting it unravel naturally. If you take time to appreciate each moment the day will seem to last so much longer, and when you review it you will find you have accomplished more than you would have expected.

Sit quietly at the beginning of your day, take in the beauties of life on earth and within, and as you stay connected to your real self you will be inspired to live according to the dictates of your heart. How often have you all gone hastily into something, expecting good results, only to find that things did not turn out as you expected?

We, therefore, say to you that in the now is the way to spend your whole day, not in meditation, of course, but with that attachment you feel in meditation to your whole being. You will have a clearer understanding of what needs to be done and you will receive all the help needed as you undertake the next stage on your pathway. If you could only see it you would be amazed, because your pathway is lit up with gold and silver light to guide you on your way. As you feel the love and light all around you make time to be aware of the conditions you are in.

'To whom much is given much is expected.' Your lives will not feel as though you have onerous tasks to perform if you stay in this glorious moment, this bubble of light and love. Then happiness, beyond comprehension, will accompany you wherever you go.

Life on Earth

We come to you this morning in love and peace, and to enjoy with you the beautiful conditions of your day, a day before most people are awake or moving, where there is stillness all around. A stillness of mind; for there is movement of wind but, within that wind, in the centre, is the Great Spirit, the Great Spirit of all things, of all beings, of all life. Without this Great Spirit there would be no life on earth, no life anywhere in the universe.

Before creation there was only the Great Spirit. Can you imagine time before creation? Well, you were there, my friends, because you have always been part of the Great Spirit and you always will be. Part of the Great Spirit? In fact, to say part is not correct as you *are* the Great Spirit. You may feel separate; the reason for your lives on earth is to feel and look as individuals, but the reality is that you, your spirit, has always been. We will leave you to meditate on this, to absorb this information, for a few minutes.

How does this make you feel? Do you feel an expansion within your heart centre? That centre of love where all actions, all activities within the human body come from – the source within. As you sit quietly and contemplate this feeling, and knowledge, you may receive a tingling, a pulsating expansion within.

We now wish to take you back in time, before this lifetime, before many, many lifetimes, when life as you know it first started on your earth. The waters were all clear, full of life; the vegetation, trees, animal life were all there from the beginning. Time allows for natural evolvement in all life and, as you, your ancestors became used to life on earth. You built homes for yourselves and gradually, over time, you were given the inspirations and inventions to improve your lives, your surroundings, your methods of trading, but as time went on you forgot who you really were.

The earth and its people have now reached a crisis, both in

relationship with one another and in their use, your use, of modern facilities and armaments for war. Your scientific knowledge in this field has reached such proportions that, at a press of a button, you could bring to an end life as you know it on earth. Your world leaders, therefore, have great responsibilities and have had so for some years. With the increase of so-called tyrants in your world, the imbalance of rich and poor nations, of plentiful and lack of food across the world, coupled with the general selfish nature of such a large proportion of your population, then yes, indeed, you have all reached crisis point.

That is why your earth needs people and groups to educate them in the ways of the spirit. There are many such groups around the world, many in their infancy and some who are ready to go forth and teach by example. As you feel the love within, so this will enable you, as you come together, to pass on the great teachings of your forefathers. These teachings are adapted to modern life and language, so continue my friends, produce the teachings so that they are readily available as the need arises and help can be given in a tangible form that will, in time, be understood by all.

You may be the embryos of the new beginning for this earth and, yes, it is a big responsibility but you have, and will have, all the help you will ever need. So, be ready, willing and we will help you to be able.

Diversity to Unity

As we come together let us feel the peace, the peace that fills the silence. The silence contains everything and yet, outwardly, appears as nothing. Nothing contains everything for all is within the Great Spirit. From your eyes it could be described as the whole universe being within this one unimaginable Spirit. It is as though all is within a magic bubble called God.

Appearances, of course, are different as you see things on your planet as separate, whereas there is only the One. You feel separate in this life, as it was intended, and there are so many experiences you can gain from this perspective. You feel, you see, hear and touch as though you are separate, but within and without you are part of the whole.

So, how does this wisdom, knowledge, call it what you may, help you all during this sojourn on earth? It is because you have the opportunity to put into practice love for God and your fellow men and women. To go from diversity to unity can only be done with the help of the Great Spirit. As you start to feel that you have this connection with all people, all beings, you experience Divine love. If you were *born* with the full understanding that you were One with God you would not experience free will and that great love for one another and all life on earth. It would be similar to God's experience before creation came into being. Only through the creation of mankind was He able to experience love.

Your scientists, with their microscopes and ever-larger telescopes keep making new discoveries, but with these new discoveries they seem to be getting further from the absolute truth. There are, of course, some within the scientific fold who believe in God, but they sometimes find it hard to reconcile their faith with the scientific results.

Where is all this leading my friends? You could describe the situation on your earth as being in the melting pot. Diversity has never been so prevalent, even in India, which is now becoming a leading industrial, commercial and highly technical nation. Their traditions for spiritual understandings are well known throughout the world and many pilgrims visit this great country for spiritual enlightenment. There is still a great tradition for religion in that country and many people follow the ancient spiritual teachings. However, it is with the general public where new temptations and experiences of wealth are happening and wealth is becoming the new god for many.

Although there is such diversity on your earth do not worry as it is in the Divine plan that you will all gradually come together, following the planned increase in vibrations and changes that will bring a wake-up call to all people. Those of you who are fortunate enough to feel the spirit within will be called upon to play your part in bringing this knowledge to the people and will help bring about the spiritual awakening on your earth.

So, my friends, be aware of the Great Spirit at all times as you are prepared for this work.

Everlasting Moment

This is the time of day when all is quiet, just before the mad rush starts.

'It is in moments like this that you can be close to Me.'

You can almost feel the very air you breathe for, although you can't see it, it is tangible and without it you would not survive in your human forms.

'Rest in this peaceful and everlasting moment, for that is all you will ever have; for it was in the moment when I created all things. It is in the moment when you create your day; it is in the moment when you can feel at the pinnacle of life. So, take time to be in that moment. You have millions of moments in your life but you can only live them one at a time. When you are aware of this moment a beautiful vista opens up from within and you feel the confidence of who you really are. You feel the love and peace all around you, as though you were at the centre of the universe, for when you are close to Me you are at the very centre of the universe.

'So, start the day being close to Me and your whole day will resound with the glories of My world. You will be at peace and My peace and love will go before you as you tread this earthly pathway, surrounded by unseen angels, who are all working to establish My will on earth.'

You, who feel this calling, will come together and establish the foundations for a new heaven on earth. You will work with the new vibrations, which are being raised at this very moment all around you. Although the majority of people are not aware of any of this they will, in time, feel the effects both on themselves and the earth, and upon everyone they meet.

You will be like beacons lighting up people's hearts, as they come to terms with the new conditions they find themselves in. That is not to say that there will be wholesale changes on earth. We are talking about the mental and emotional changes that will occur in the minds of people on the earth. The effects will vary depending upon individual pathways and progress and the work that they will be doing to readjust to this glorious new way of life.

People will at first feel lost, and lacking confidence, as so much will be changing in the political and business scenes and in everyday life. Those who have strong values will take the changes in their stride and, although others may find it more difficult, you beacons of light will be there to help as you explain and bring love, God's love, with you in all you do and say.

So, be very happy and content, knowing that we are with you, encouraging you to fulfil your part of the Divine plan.

The Sound of Silence

We come to you today with love and peace, and as we settle in with you, you will notice the sound of silence. Everything develops from the sound of silence for it is in this silence that you are able to be at One with the Father of all life. In the silence everything seems still and yet, the God within, that pulsating powerhouse, is not only in all beings but also throughout the entire universe.

What a statement, my friends! Can anyone really take in this profound truth? To experience and stay in this closeness, being at One with All That Is, is the most peaceful, yet stirring, challenging and incredulous realisation that you are part of and, indeed, within all life. Your soul, or consciousness, can understand this but your very nature and conditioning make it very hard to understand and accept. You can, and do, feel the love and connection within and when you stay in this moment you are touching everything, my friends, and experiencing the wonders of the One Mind.

As you feel your heart expand so your consciousness will ever widen, for consciousness is the spirit's outer shell or soul. Stay in this all-encompassing, glorious light of God, where all wisdom and truth can be found. The history of all life is within you at all times if you could only be in it, being in the love, the aura of the Father. By saying 'be in it' we mean *experience* it, for in truth God's aura covers all life, both physical and spiritual and you cannot go anywhere where God is not. So, take this glorious experience of Divinity with you as you go through your day. Make a point of feeling that *beingness* from time to time and your stature, showing as confidence, love and willingness to serve, will go before you as you continue on life's journey, that destiny which is known within but is difficult to know in the mind.

When you are aware of this consciousness life opens up to you in ways unthought-of and undreamed of and you will, indeed, become aware of your chosen pathway in this beautiful and exciting life that is ahead of you all. So, come regularly to your Father within to explore the beauties and challenges of this wonderful life on earth.

At the Ready

Do you feel 'at the ready' and what does it mean?

You can feel at the ready for something you are about to do but in the context of being ready with your God then it simply means being ready to accept that your God is within you, ready to feel and be aware of this. You have read about this truth, heard about it, and now is the time to experience it.

When you start your day it is good to have a little time alone and feel at One with All That Is. You may not have any feelings to begin with but, believe me, if the intention is there then you are at One with your God. The light is all around you, even if you cannot see it, just as the peace is within and around you also. So, relax into this communion with your God. It helps, of course, to leave all one's usual thoughts outside at this time, or if they do enter your consciousness then let them travel in and out of you, without letting them take up residence.

You can stay in this beautiful state as long or as short a time as you wish. You will find that it becomes easier to go within as you persevere with it. Not only does it, or will it, feel peaceful and awe-inspiring but the effects it has throughout your whole body are quite amazing. Your vital organs are penetrated with light and love, giving energy and vigour from within. The longer you stay in this peaceful and rewarding state the more love you will receive, which will pass through your bodies and to all you may come in contact with during your day.

This profound truth will serve you well in the days ahead as you come together in love and peace, ready to carry out your life's plan and continue on the pathway designed by and for you at this time. You will be ready and feel confident that you will not only deal with life's challenges but you will come to relish them and enjoy the situations that will occur.

Take time to appreciate the beauty and power within as you are transformed with a confidence, peace and stature that will go before you and enable you all to take on the mantle of teachers in this world, where the need is ever greater for spiritual knowledge. You have been chosen for this work and know that you have been prepared for it a long time ago.

So, you will be ready for all the knowledge, love and light that will be at your disposal when necessary. Take time then, my friends, to start the day in this way, and from time to time go within, and your day will be full and rewarding as you go through life with God at your side.

Note: The following quotation for 25 March is from Eileen Caddy's daily message book *Opening Doors Within*. It underlines and is analogous with the main points of this teaching.

As more and more love is released into the world, a wonderful healing is taking place. It is like balm poured into wounds, healing and making whole. Love starts with the individual. It starts in you, and it grows like a seed, bursting forth revealing great beauty and wholeness. It is what is taking place now. Many souls feel that something is happening to them, but they are bewildered and do not realise what it is. They search without, hoping to find a clue which will show them what is taking place. Other souls feel a stirring but are afraid of what they feel, for it is new, it is strange and unknown, and they try to shut it out. Nothing will be able to stop this release of love. It is the genie in the bottle; having been released, it cannot be put back again. It cannot be hidden or ignored. Gradually it will begin to reveal itself in everyone. It has come to stay.

Re-Awakening

It is the time of day when the light is returning and all life is re-awakening from sleep. It is also now time for a re-awakening of the spiritual in people. Over the ages there have been many times when people have forgotten who they really are and, indeed, have been more interested in the physical than the spiritual. Such a time is now when man has made huge advances in technology and all aspects of the material life. If man had made similar advances in his spiritual life then the Golden Age would have already arrived.

Instead, relationships within families, friends, acquaintances, business, religion and politics, nationally and internationally, have often broken down, resulting in continued tension throughout the world. It appears that, in some areas, your unconditional love for life is often absent and, in fact, the opposite is quite prevalent. You still fight, have wars for religious reasons, and the treatment and care, not only of the aged but also for some of the animal kingdom, leaves a lot to be desired.

This, of course, does not apply to all people as the great majority have love and goodwill in their hearts but the general trend in life today on your planet has deteriorated to the point where radical action is needed to restore life to the original Divine plan for it. How is this to be done?

There are little changes afoot on your earth where the vibrations of the earth itself and all life, including people, are being raised. This will hardly be noticed at first except by the sensitive ones who are in touch with their inner selves. They know within that they will be used to help bring love, understanding and peace to all people. Within everyone there will be a light where the cells are gradually illuminated, resulting in a feeling that their bodies are slightly lighter.

Those who have the understanding, and feel this lightness within, will notice subtle changes around them, both in the earth itself and the atmosphere, where purity of the air breathed in will gradually be felt. Certain countries have already made their own efforts in this direction and they, and other countries, will be assisted to speed up the process so that there will be a cleansing within that will also manifest itself in the world.

Many of you will realise that you have been waiting for this time and you will get together in small groups to assist people to come to terms with the higher vibrations as these become stronger over time. People generally will be affected by having a feeling, or need, to change their lives and their outlook on life in order to adjust to these changes. So, help will be given to all people through the ones who come together, knowing it is their life purpose to teach and generally show the way forward by example.

We, therefore, say to all of you that the changes will be very gradual and, by being in touch with your Divine inner being, you will receive all the help needed to perform the tasks ahead in this wonderful adventure as the beginning of the Golden Age commences on your earth.

Stepping-Stones

Stepping-stones are in front of you at all times as you traverse this human life. Even as a child you wished to make progress from crawling to standing and to walking and running. So, too, within you is that desire to find the truth of who you are, why you are here, and where you are going.

In life these questions have various answers for different people, for you all have disparate personalities. You are all unique and yet you are all as One in the Great Spirit. Have you ever wondered what drives you on in this life to do things you didn't think you were capable of? Well, by taking one more step in faith enables you to achieve results not deemed possible by you only a short time previously.

Your scientists have made great strides in trying to answer the question of how life started, and they recognise the closeness of all life through DNA, but they never seem to consider the truth that you are spirit within a body, which is, in fact, true for all life. This is the missing ingredient they are looking for, but they are looking in the wrong direction. For you who realise there is more to life than the physical, and have open minds, you can accept the truth that you are all spirit. So, while the scientists carry on with their probing and investigation, you, my friends, are in the fortunate position of knowing the answer.

How to pass on this information? It is not easy and until one is open and ready for this truth people shun away from spiritual teachings. However, things are changing on your earth, as you know, with the vibrations increasing both on the earth and in its people and, indeed, in all life. For it is the way your whole being resonates with all life that determines the vibrations of the individual and the whole. All living things vibrate at different rates and can be seen by us as colours, twinkling. This is separate from the colours of the aura, which are fluctuating continuously, depending upon the health, activities, thoughts and actions of the individual.

The vibrations, my friends, on the other hand, originate through the Spirit and can be felt sometimes as a tingling in the human body when one is attuned to All That Is. As the vibrations are increased so more and more people will feel this tingling, and other effects, as your bodies become lighter than previously. This is a gradual process so most people will feel nothing initially then, as time progresses, subtle changes will appear within their lives and, of course, throughout the whole world.

Take courage then and be happy that all is as it should be and according to the Divine plan for your wonderful earth. Stay with it my friends, and you will feel these subtle changes. As you come closer to your real selves so will you be playing your part in the preparations of the Golden Age which will gradually unfold before you all.

The Truth Within

Stay a while in peace, my friends, as you take in the wonders of the universe within. Do you feel an expansion within your heart? Does it feel warm and glowing?

Then you really have within you the source, the essence of all life. You have heard these teachings before but the question is, have you felt them?

For, to let them in one ear and out of the other one is only giving scant regard to the truth; the truth that God is within you, within all of us and all of us within God. This is such an overwhelming statement that most people cannot take it on board fully and certainly not the first time they hear it. One usually thinks, oh yes, that is for others not for me; how can it be? It doesn't feel like it and, in any case, how could it possibly be true?

Well, my friends, we are telling you, as others have said before, that it is not only true but when you are fully open to this wisdom then you will feel it within every cell of your body for that is where the Lord resides. You may feel your whole body expanding as you let the absorption sink in, so that your minds can receive this truth and perceive what it really means. Many people cannot face this truth: they may half believe it for, if it is true, then we are all co-creators with the one Almighty God.

We know you may feel restricted, being in a human body, but do you think God is restricted? No, my friends! You can feel so close at times to the One Spirit within and, as you become able to touch on this awareness, then you will find that this closeness, this feeling of Oneness becomes more frequent for you until it becomes permanent. We are not saying this will become permanent immediately but it is possible, anything is possible, when you are that close to All That Is.

However, closeness is still, shall we say, only halfway to becoming completely at One with All That Is. So, contemplate on this, feel the wonder of the message, take it into your daily lives and you will see such beauty in your world. You will be looking at everything with different eyes, from a different perspective, for you will be seeing things with the eyes of God.

Live in Love and Peace

We come to you today in love and peace, bringing you greater understandings to be shared with all mankind. We start with yourselves for that is the only place to start, in your heart of hearts, where you meet your Divine Parent.

Do make time to open yourselves to All That Is at this important time in the earth's history. It is also an auspicious time for you, my friends, as you realise there is more to life than appears on the surface. As you go about your daily business look at everything anew, look into a rose, look into someone's eyes; feel the air around you for everything contains that love from God, which can be yours when you see everything in God's light.

'Start the day with love, fill the day with love, end the day with love'.

That is the secret to a wonderful and rewarding life.

'Come to Me and be fed with My love for it is free and always available. All you have to do is be sincere and open to this love. You can receive it direct or through other people who are open channels for My love. Relax completely and you will feel your whole body filled with My energy as you expand in love. As you go through life feel this love within, for it pervades all life. Those in touch with this power or energy will recognise it in others, as it returns to Me and creates an ever-widening circle of beings that are aware of My love at all times.

'You all have the potential to become great ones, Masters, when you are continually aware of My love coming through and in you, to inspire and uplift not only you but also all you meet, whether they are people, animals or the vegetable kingdom. All life has My energy flowing through it and when you recognise this you will have the opportunity to become at One with all life.

'It is a great time in your lives when you know that you are more than just flesh and bones, that you hold within you the essence and truth to establish the foundation for a new way of life on earth. You have all been chosen for this task, so step forward in the light and be guided as you come together in peace. You will bring forth My message to all mankind to live together in love and peace and hear the truth that I AM in the tiniest drop of rain, in the molecules that make up the very air you breathe, in the blood that flows through your veins, and from everything you see and touch to everything you cannot see, but know is there, to ensure the continuance of life as you know it.

'So, take these words, given to mankind since time immemorial, into your souls and let them reside there as you come to terms with the purpose and future direction of your lives.'

You, who have been honoured to receive these words, have the opportunity to make a change, not only in your own lives but to all those around you in the days ahead, as you live your lives according to the dictates of your hearts, knowing the love of All That Is is with you, in you and around you at all times.

The Narrow or Wide Road

It used to be thought that the narrow road was the way to God; narrow in the sense of living one's life in solitude and meeting as few people as possible. While it is true that it is still one pathway to God the best way by far in this modern age is to be *in* but not *of* the world. In other words to be living, meeting and joining people in their activities, while still being on your own for some of the time, without being attached to all the material trappings of life. To be with people shows them, by example, what it means to have God in one's heart, talking about it, being happy and at One with all things, all nature, all people, but above all being at One with your God.

For people who follow this pathway knowing that God is within not only themselves but in all people, all beings, all nature and in all inanimate objects, will change their attitude and give them opportunities to look at their own lives. To have the courage to make changes so that one is living according to the feelings within will seem strange at first but, as you get used to this, it will become automatic and you will not need to think about it as you will just *be* as you dedicate your life to God; for you are with God and God is with you and all people.

As you move through life with this love within it will feel like riding on the crest of a wave where you are taken along, having risen above all the petty arguments and distractions of the material side of life. This does not mean you will be aloof in any way; in fact you will appear to others as down to earth, with a confidence and glow within you, shown in your face and manner. Love will exude from you in the way you are, and when people need you for advice you will be there. You will be in their hearts as they think of you when they have problems.

You will stand out as beings of light and people will feel your magnetism and will want to be near you. This means you will have a big responsibility but it won't feel like that to you, for being in touch with your real self ensures any help needed will be readily available. So, to you who will be carrying the light at this very auspicious time, we say that you should continue feeling love and peace within, as the ancient truths are given to you to pass on to all whom you meet. You will be examples when the earth is going through changes, also from within, and in time these changes will be reflected without, for the increasing vibrations will not only be felt by the people but also by the very planet you live on.

Take stock then, my friends. You who have been chosen for this work will come together with like-minded people and, as the wisdom is bestowed upon you all, so you will then go your separate ways to the four corners of the earth. You will be the ones to explain the reasons for the changes taking place and, as more and more people come to you for advice and help to meet the new challenges, so you will find all the help you need within, as you live in this circle of love which extends before you as you follow the natural promptings from the Divine within.

My friends, this may seem a little beyond the pale, so to speak, but believe me this will happen and you are being prepared daily for the tasks ahead. You will feel your bodies becoming lighter, resulting in a gradual ease of movement, not felt by you since your childhood. Use this free-flowing wondrous energy to enjoy life, for you will be in touch with all of nature. You will feel that you are part of all and that you will be in the very cells of all beings.

At the same time you will be living a normal life to all intents and purposes. Nothing will have really changed, except that you will have come of age, as you all prepare the way for the coming of the new Golden Age on earth.

Microscopic World

Your scientists today live in a microscopic world as their investigations into life put greater and greater emphasis on the smallest particle or sub-atomic particle in the world.

Although they think they have found the building blocks of life as it originated on your earth they are, in the main, searching in a material way rather than in a spiritual manner. Discoveries will, of course, continue to be made, but until scientists work hand in hand with spiritual channels they will never accept the truth that God is at the heart of all, from the tiniest atom to the whole universe: for all life, from microcosm to macrocosm, is God. As above so below, microcosm to macrocosm, all has basically the same make-up, which started when the Great Mind, Almighty God, created everything so long, long ago.

There is reason behind all creation and although, for example, most of the planets in your solar system do not appear to have life as you know it they are, nevertheless, there for a purpose. In the Divine plan, your God, the One and only God, created the perfect world and, of course, the universe, which is forever pulsating and recreating itself as life continues to evolve wherever it may be.

My friends, when you are in deep meditation you are at the heart of God and it is only your mind that prevents you from experiencing the indescribable wholeness and beauty of All That Is. It can be experienced within as true bliss, an incredible feeling that you are One in the centre of greatness surrounded by universal love. This is called 'being in the moment' for that moment of glory and perfection could last forever. For most people who have this amazing moment it is like enlightenment, but the mind comes in and the moment is lost.

The enormity of enlightenment cannot be truly expressed and only happens with the grace of God. You do not have to chase after it for, when the time is right, it will just happen. However, everyone can experience or have a sense of it in their regular meditation and quiet times.

So, take the peace, the joy and the love that you can experience into your lives and the light from your auras will shine before you and around you as you perform your daily duties. Once you have touched upon this enlightenment your lives will never feel the same, as you will have deep peace surrounding you.

Your normal activities will still continue and with your newfound confidence, peace and unconditional love you will feel that you are floating through life, just touching the soft ground as you spend your time in service to mankind in one way or another.

Much has been said and written about enlightenment and it really is just a natural progression into communion with All That Is.

The Storehouse Within

To be at peace requires strength of mind to go within where all is contained. That is to say, you all have within you all the resources necessary to live a peaceful and perfect life. It is a storehouse provided by the Almighty for our use. You may use it often, ignore it, or only use it from time to time. However, for whatever reason you think you are using it, the real purpose is to help you carry out your chosen pathway. Many people are not aware of this but they can, without realising it, still be inspired when appropriate. For those who are aware, it provides the security of a so-called backup of all knowledge, energy and power during one's life journey.

We are here to help you bring out this wonderful facility, which you have within, to inspire and take forth with you in your daily life. Not only is it a storehouse but the more you use it the more of it then becomes available to you, just as love is always replaced in this way. You are, or will be, able to feel this energy and love within as a warm glow, so rest in it for it is a gift from the Almighty that few people are presently aware of.

However, as the vibrations increase on the earth, more and more people will be enquiring as to the purpose of their life and will come to hear of this wonderful knowledge that all, yes everything, is within and can be reached when one is ready to receive. It may be difficult at first but if you stay with it, even for just short periods, you will find the energy, the love, within. You will find the truth of your being, so remain there and you will go deeper, although you may not at first be aware of what is happening. Your whole being will be enveloped in this glorious light for, once found, it is always there ready to be tapped into and will assist you in your everyday life and especially for the purpose, the reason, that you are on the earth plane.

So, immerse yourself in this love and light whenever you are able, and particularly in the morning and evening as you find a little quiet time. This will help you for the rest of the day, as an everlasting peace grows within and throughout you.

Those of you who are willing, and who find their true selves within, will have the opportunity to join the growing band of like-minded people being prepared to take the earth and its peoples to the next stage of its evolution. You will come together in love, and work for the benefit of all mankind as you are inspired to take the next step yourselves.

It will seem as natural as night follows day that everything will fall into place at the right time, as you meet people on the same pathway. You will come together to be inspired, and prepared, to embrace the ancient teachings as a way of life that assists all mankind, rather than everyone only working for their own ends.

You will know, by having a strong feeling of well-being, that you are making a difference to enable future generations to live in peace and harmony, when the earth's riches will enable all to have sufficient food and poverty becomes a thing of the past. The more you share and work for each other the more will become available, as the Lord has provided enough reserves for everyone to live comfortably.

So, go in peace my friends, safe in the knowledge that the Divine plan is well and truly in motion to create the long-awaited Golden Age in due time for all to share.

I AM

I AM All That Is, all that you can see, feel, hear, all that you
can know, all that ever was, is and ever will be.

I AM the sound, the light, I AM the sea, the land. I AM.

I AM All That Is. You see Me in all life. There is nowhere that
I AM not. You feel Me within and I AM with you always.

Most people are not aware of this truth, the truth that
everything arises from Me. Everything has its foundation
in Me.

I AM in the very air you breathe, in the space all around you.

I AM above, below, within. I AM.

As you contemplate on Me let go and let God into your lives.

For the truth is that I AM in your lives always.

I AM in the smallest atom, within the atom, within the space
in the atom, within the protons, neutrons and electrons.
I AM in the furthest star in the universe.

I do not push Myself on you because I AM in you. I AM you.

My love for you is endless. As you feel Me within, and let
yourselves expand with the enormity of My message,
remember Me and be Me every moment of your day,
for I AM with you always and share in all your thoughts,
words and deeds.

I feel your love, your aches and pains, your happiness, your
unhappiness, your enthusiasm, and your zest for life.

I AM the Life for I will always be and you will, too. So feel
Me, see Me and hear Me throughout your life.

I AM your Guide, your Father, Mother, Lover and Friend.

I AM Everywhere

I AM in the gentlest breeze, in the strongest gale, in the calm and peaceful waters and the raging sea.

I AM in your heart; your heart is in Me. I see and hear your every move, from the slightest tapping of your finger to the loudest banging on the drum.

I AM everywhere.

I AM your soul, your spirit. I AM your body.

I AM the air you breathe; I AM the cloud, the rain and snow, the mist and the brilliant sunshine.

I AM the world, the universe.

I just AM.

I AM One with All

'I AM One with All'. Take this saying into your heart, into the soul of your body, for once there it resonates throughout every cell in you, and that will be your natural state.

My friends, as you sit in meditation and go ever inwards you touch on that infinite love, that love that can change anything. That love that can transform the darkest image into the brightest light, for it is the basis of all life. Take that love with you into whatever problems you may have in the day. Just pause and think of this infinite love and you will be helped through your problems. No one can take away your problems as they are part and parcel of your life, your pathway, but being in tune with the infinite love of your Father God enables you to ride over them skilfully, with an energy that confidently turns problems into opportunities.

Opportunities for love in action are why you are really on this earth, to experience and instigate them. It can be in the smallest action, a smile for someone in distress or a kind thought, for there are always opportunities in your life if you are aware of your surroundings. Even if you are at home, and do not go out, you are still able to send out that love in action as you think of people in distress or who just need some support.

You have telephones and many have internet or e-mail to make contact. Take the opportunity to ring people who are lonely and may need help or encouragement. You have all received contact in this way and it has lifted your spirits, so be aware and ready to serve in this way when the possibility is in your heart and mind. There are so many ways you can serve, my friends, and when you are ready and able the occasions will be there for you. In fact, as in all things, the more you do the more opportunities will there be for you.

You don't even have to tell anyone, enquire of anybody or write to anyone. When your heart and mind offer themselves then it will be taken up and opportunities will present themselves, not necessarily in the way you envisaged, because there are so many different and countless ways to choose from, but there will be one or more just for you. Your pathway will become clearer and you will know instinctively which avenue to take. That is not to say you are restricting yourself to any one way to help, but in order to be most effective you cannot take on every task in the world either. So, be at One, my friends, and you will be aware of the avenues to take to be most useful in your service to mankind.

Love is not a commodity but an all-encompassing force from God. When helping in any way you are passing on this wondrous love. You cannot store it within but the more you give out the more you receive, so you don't need an invisible bank account. You may use your last drop but it will be replaced a hundredfold and you will never lack from the source of love. Feel this love, use it, and pray for opportunities to give it out as you go through life. You will never be without this love yourselves as it will be in you and around you waiting to be replaced as more is sent on its way.

You, my friends, who live a life of love in action, will never need anything as the love that comes through you on its way to others leaves a lasting mark within you. Your hearts and souls will feel energised and full of happiness and lasting peace which will be felt by others as they come in contact with you.

Therefore, dwell a while in this love and peace and be ready at any time to link into this wondrous feeling within, in preparation for all those opportunities that lie ahead.

Part Five

Putting the Teachings into Practice

The Living Planet

Your planet is, indeed, living. It was created by the One Great Spirit; it moves, breathes, feels and has spirit within, as does all life. This helps nature regenerate and recover from, what you would call, disasters and man-made explosions and experiments beneath its surface.

It is balanced like a precision instrument and is like clockwork when finely tuned. However, when it is knocked off balance it reacts in ways that you have come to expect, weather extremes with more hurricanes and differing seasons plus earthquakes and volcanoes erupting. With all the hammering it takes from mankind it is still performing the will of God and will continue to do so for many, many eons. It is up to mankind to repair the damage caused over many years by his ill-treatment of the earth.

My friends, please lead the way in showing it love and tender care as you would a member of your family or friend. The earth is a living being and will respond to this love in a most positive way.

Your scientists and politicians are making noises and having some effect by endeavouring to reduce the amount of carbon dioxide produced every day. While this is admirable, it is the love and healing from mankind that will help restore it to its true beauty and status.

Your ancient forefathers used to pray to, and revere, the sun, earth and nature. Although we are not suggesting you treat them as gods and worship them, we do ask you to love the earth and become one with it in the manner that you are trying to be at One with the Great Spirit within.

Unseen Colours

You are pure light within and to us you all shine at different levels. We can tell by thought and your auric colours who you are. These range from the dullest brown to the brightest purple, and encompassing all the colours is the pure white of Spirit. We can also see that you are all connected by this light and can tell, for instance, if you are worried or anxious as the colours are dimmed, whereas when you are relaxed, happy and enthusiastic the colours emanating from you are clear and vibrant.

We are aware of prayers, healing thoughts and love giving bright colours and also negative thoughts, such as jealousy or hatred, which put a totally different hue on them. So, my friends, beautiful colours and dull ones are all intermingled as you go through your day and you often notice negative or positive thoughts as you meet with each other.

Although it is rare for one to see the aura you are, nevertheless, able to sense things as you go through life. You may converse with each other and may pick up signals to give a hint of how truthful the words really are. In most cases this perception is not normally present, but as one becomes more in tune with the real self then you will find that this gift increases. We are not suggesting that you should lead your life being suspicious of everything that is said to you, but just to be aware if you have a feeling that all is not right in any communication.

Your light, when strong, goes before you and acts as a protection when you are in certain difficult situations. So, lead from the front, feeling your spirit within, and you will be able to shrug off any negativity that you encounter on your journey.

Friend

Who are my friends? First and foremost the One Great Spirit within all life, and that is really the only answer.

When on earth we used to worship the tall trees that reached for the sun during the day and reached for the stars at night. We worshipped the sun, for it gave warmth and beauty to the earth. We worshipped the moon, for it showed us direction at night and shone with its silvery light on the sea and rivers. We worshipped the animals and revered all life.

Now that we have greater understanding we are helping our friends on earth to understand the meaning of life. The simple ways in life seem to have been lost with the growing of ever larger cities and modern technology.

We ask you all to look at nature. The tree still stands proud and searches for light; the grass is still rich and is food for the animals. The flowers, too numerous to count, still adorn God's landscape on earth; their seeds and resultant vegetation still provide essential food. Nature provided sustenance for all life in abundance and was always self-sufficient until man interfered by clearing forests and changing the make-up of plants, nowadays called genetically modified.

They say a little knowledge is a dangerous thing, and this is where some of your scientists and leaders think they are solving starvation on earth. While their sentiments are good they are misguided as the Great Spirit originally provided perfection and order on earth, with purity of water in the rivers, sea, soil and resultant food, whereas now they are polluted and disease is prolific in all areas of life.

So, my friends look for purity, starting within and in all life, for that is where the supreme Spirit resides. Make way for spirit in your hearts and revere spirit in all people, animals and life, including the land and all that grows therein, the fish in the sea and water itself. It is by having awareness of, and worshipping, the Great Spirit within all life that will eventually return your planet to its rightful order and purity.

The Continuity of Life

Where are you going? What is important to you in this life? Where is it leading?

These are questions that you must have asked at some time or other. For one solitary life without continuance, either before or afterward, cannot make any sense. You were born without any knowledge of teachings and previous experiences and yet, within your souls, this knowledge is held and waiting to be unlocked as you progress through this life and when the time is right for you.

When you hear or read spiritual teachings they sometimes resonate with you so strongly it is as though you had heard them before. Other teachings may be rejected by you without any real reason, and you might wonder why this is. The truth, my friends, is that certain teachings are recognised by your spirit or soul. The spirit and soul are closely linked, but different, the spirit being the purity of All That Is and the soul containing your memories i.e. your past and also your future hopes and destiny. Yes! You have, in some form or other, always existed and the secrets of your previous adventures that have moulded your awareness are locked within your soul. When you are ready the key will open up and reveal some of these secrets.

Firstly, a feeling of being connected to all life will occur, followed by a desire for spiritual knowledge. Then, as you go through life more truths will open up to you and, depending upon your life's plan, you will know within what you need to know to fulfil your life on earth. Some people have little or no recollection of the greater understanding of life, while others have no doubt that life is eternal.

It would not be appropriate to remember your past lives while still in this one. There are exceptions, but in the main you don't remember, otherwise it could have an adverse effect on your current life, as would knowing how long your present life would be. Your experiences are more meaningful without this sort of information. Most of you hope for life after death and there are, today, more and more people who are coming to realise that life is, indeed, eternal for all. There are no exceptions, so, for example, someone deciding to end their own life would find themselves waking up on our side of life.

Whatever type of life one has led there is no exception, as all will find themselves alive after so-called death. This comes as a shock for many and it sometimes takes a long time for them to adjust to their new surroundings. Others, who have a strong belief and knowing, find the transition beautiful, quick and easy. They soon adjust to their new life and all will eventually realise that they have not died.

It is true that the life you lead on earth has a strong bearing on the circumstances you find yourself in when you traverse to the next life. Therefore, when you have an opportunity to read spiritual truths that resonate with you then do explore this more fully so that when it is your time to pass to the higher life you will find yourself in familiar conditions when met by your loved ones.

Gamesmanship

For those acquainted with sport this is an area where gamesmanship is not exactly cheating, but is nearly so, with one side displaying delaying tactics, etc., the intention being to put off one's opponent and so remove the level playing field with which the game started.

Sport is a recreation liked by so many people and the purpose is, surely, to enjoy the game as you pit yourselves against one another. So, to employ gamesmanship of any kind is to obstruct the free-flowing enjoyment of all participants when it is intended that the game be played by fair means. My friends, gamesmanship has familiarities with all of life's contests. Reducing them to unfair activities often results in frustration, and even anger, when participants feel unjustly treated.

When sports were invented there were no rules made for gamesmanship and the same applies to relationships, politics, business and social aspects of life. Your political contests, elections, seem to be more about criticising and digging up degrading information on one's opponent, rather than expounding upon one's own policies.

Where is all this leading us, my friends? When opponents in sport, or other activities, are spending more time on gamesmanship than on its real purpose then once again it is symptomatic of what is happening today all over your planet. Until people take a good look at themselves and ask who they really are, what they are here for and where their lives are leading, then change will not take place.

The One God is within all life, which means that His Spirit is within all of you. When this is realised what would be the point of employing unfair tactics against your opponent, who also has the same God within him or her. It puts a totally different light on the situation and, as one of the reasons you are here is to find your real self within, then all this unfair behaviour will only delay your happy reunion with God within.

How life on the earth would change overnight if everyone was aware of this truth as it would also enable one to follow their own personal Divine plan.

Conditions on Earth

We come to you with open arms and hearts, offering you our love unreservedly as we look at conditions on earth today.

The industrial power of nations is changing. Your financial markets have had a problematic time and there has been little overall growth in commercial and industrial activities.

Why do the leaders of governments and industries always expect continued growth in sales and output? They have been used to it since the industrial revolution and their businesses are geared to ever-increasing profits. There is never any satisfaction in standing still as it is a human trait to always look for more. However, when this is achieved, to the detriment of their workers and competitors, it is symptomatic of today's standards on earth. Providing care for one another tends to disappear when there is a continual pursuit of profits at all costs.

This attitude has spread to all areas of life today, for example, in the political scene. It appears that most people have lost sight of why they are on the earth and, unless there is a total change in outlook across the board, there will be far-reaching consequences. People have had their fill of this way of life and are looking for help and inspiration.

The earth is being flooded with love and peaceful vibrations at this time, and those of you who are sensitive will begin to feel the changes at the heart of all life. More and more will stop and question where their lives are going and, indeed, what life is all about and why they are here. You will feel a change within as you go about your normal lives and the opportunities will be there for business and political leaders to make a change in fundamental working relationships.

Many will want to join a growing band of people and groups throughout the world who will help explain the changes that are taking place. They will encourage people to look for more in their lives of a spiritual nature. Gradually these changes will permeate through industry and all walks of life. People will tend toward a cheery, optimistic disposition rather than a pessimistic, depressed view of life, which has been all too common of late.

So, those of you who are aware of the changing, higher vibrations on earth will be shown within how you can help start to bring in the long-awaited new Golden Age on your earth.

Your World

We join you today in love and peace and joy as you prepare to face the world you know for another day. The world you know is unique to each one of you as it is encompassed within your whole being. You may think your whole world is your house, community and your friends and acquaintances, etc. but, on its own, it seems a tiny part of the world.

In fact your world is as small or large as you wish it to be. If you embrace the whole world in your mind then your thoughts, your caring, your love will have far-reaching effects, whereas if your world stays just in your little community then the thoughts, goodwill and love stay there. So, open up your hearts and minds to infinity and there will be no restriction on how far your love can extend. This is all done from within, my friends, that special place where you can go to be at One with your spirit. From here there is no end to where you can go. As you reach this state feel your whole body relax into deep, deep peace.

Now, your world expands in love and beauty beyond description. If you stay a while in this state your prayers, your thoughts for the welfare of all life will traverse the continents and be used to help bring, or maintain, peace in troubled areas around the world. So, you see, my friends, from a small local view it is transformed to a global view when your heart, mind and soul are in tune with the Great Spirit. In this moment all life's adventures can begin.

You now include all life as you feel at One and have this expanding feeling within. Your view of life will change forever as you go forward in your life's plan to enjoy and experience all that goes before you, knowing that you can return at any time to this space, this wondrous God-given space where you can truly feel at home in your world.

Love

Eternal truth is timeless, for in whatever age wisdom is the same. It may vary in the way it is taught or explained, but at the heart of all wisdom is love. Love, that unseen gift of God is behind the very foundation of life on earth. The love of the Father can be felt everywhere from the air you breathe to the little robin that sits on the garden spade. The love within all life is dominant, being a force that enables movement and action on your planet.

Although love itself cannot be seen the effects of it can, and when one looks for the positive actions of people, rather than the negative ones, all manner of kindness and caring is continually taking place. How could it be otherwise when the essence of God's love is within you all? 'Ah', we hear you say, 'How can God's love be in terrorists, murderers, criminals, etc.?'

We assure you that God's love is, indeed, within all people, including the ones just mentioned. Although their deeds do not show the love you would expect it is still inherent within them, buried deep where an apparent shield, produced by conditioning, etc. and blind faith in unusual ideals, seems to cover it up for the time being.

Jesus taught 'love thy enemies' as He preached the ancient truth that God is within all life. Love begets love, as like attracts like, and to see some good within so-called outcasts of society can have surprising results. There is no evil in this life, just misguided directions and inclinations. We are not advocating that punishment for bad deeds in your society is wrong as this is a consequence of the natural law of cause and effect. What we are saying is follow the Master's teachings of loving God and all mankind, including ones enemies.

Love does not mean being soft but instead, caring and educating in such a way that these people have the opportunity to look at their lives anew and make a clean start. Rather than looking for the results of love let it be instigated into your lives and show it to all mankind, regardless of misdeeds and appearances. Generally, man seems to have forgotten to love unconditionally and society is crying out for a peaceful revolution in relationships with one another.

When the love of the Father is given by mankind unreservedly to all it will be the antidote to all the troubles in your world today.

Embrace all Life

To embrace all life is to carry out the will of the Great Spirit. You are all One within the Great Mind and, although physically you all appear and feel separate, you are all connected and are, therefore, one with each other and the Lord God.

This Oneness can be felt when you give yourself time to sit quietly in prayer and thanksgiving to the One Great Spirit. However, you normally appear to one another as individuals in the vast apparent diversity of all life. As such you all have unique Divine life plans and it is when you are following, or are close to, this plan on your journey that this feeling of Oneness will surround you.

One of the biggest causes of disharmony in life today is that of judgement of your fellow brothers and sisters. When one is aware of the great truth of Oneness there is no longer a reason to judge. However, during the course of your normal daily lives there are many occurrences where you feel aggrieved, individually or collectively, for one reason or another. It is at these times, therefore, that by remembering or feeling the Oneness of all life that the tendency to judge can be tempered, or removed, with the great love of the Father within.

So, whenever you can, in your busy days, take time to sit and dwell on the Oneness of all as you come to embrace life anew with the love, peace and joy of the spirit within.

New Relationships

May the Lord God be with you as we join you in love and homage to the Great Spirit. We are mindful of His great love for all life; the Great Spirit's love surrounds, penetrates and is within all at all times. When we are aware of this, and can link into that great truth and feeling, then there is nothing that cannot be achieved, for this love has no barriers and can repair any broken relationships, make new ones and allow people to develop their own love for one another.

Today so many relationships have broken down in all walks of life, in governments and internationally. Your world leaders put on a pretence of bringing God into their relationships but, unfortunately, most of them have their own priorities which tend to stifle sensible and satisfactory agreements or treaties with one another. Such are the relationships with so many people, individuals and business; their own demands are prioritised, rather than searching for the good of all in any situation. Well, my friends, this really can't go on for history tells of continual wars on your earth. A completely new look at relationships will be necessary before long-term peace and love throughout the land is forthcoming.

For a start, it is evident that the majority of people want to live a peaceful life but the tendency has been, in the main, for them to look after 'number one' and forget others who may be in a less fortunate position.

There are groups throughout the world who have given up their own way of life to assist others, both in raising money and giving practical help to those in need. This is truly admirable and is, in the main, producing grand results.

However, a complete change in most people's lives and outlook will be necessary to produce far-reaching and long-lasting conditions on the earth that will lead to a joyous and warm relationship between all people. It appears that very few are aware of, and want to make, these changes. Therefore, it is those who are ready, with love in their hearts and a desire to put the good of others before themselves, who will come together, slowly at first, improving the conditions around them by their love, devotion and willingness to do whatever is necessary at this time.

There are pockets of such people willing and able to carry out their life's plan in this way. They will be led in the days ahead and, for the time being, their coming together in love and peace is already having an effect on the conditions surrounding your planet. As time proceeds, those involved will know what to do in bringing a new way of life to your world, gradually at first, but then the appetite of people everywhere will change as they become ready to listen to, and put into practice, the teachings that will be given to them.

So, we say to you, feel that love of the Great One within you and all around you, connecting to your real selves so that you can carry out your life's work in the knowledge that you will be following the Divine will.

With the light surrounding you, and help that will always be available, a peaceful revolution will take place as the new Golden Age becomes a reality.

The Purpose of Life

You sit in contemplation of your God in the peace and love that is so conducive for this purpose. The creatures of the sea all have purpose, as do the animals, the insects and all life on the earth. How much more then is the purpose of mankind? It is, indeed, a great privilege to spend time on the earth to experience life in the physical, which cannot be felt anywhere else.

So, with gratitude in your heart and love for your fellow man you will be living out the purpose of your incarnation. That is, to find out who you really are and use the information to spend your life in service to mankind. This is the best way to experience the love of your Father. Look for Him in all life and you will start to feel within a tender relationship with everyone you meet. Look for the good in people and you will see through the outer façade to the very centre of their being, where the Lord resides.

You will find that when you look at people anew, with an inner love for them, there will be recognition of closeness toward each other. This may not show outwardly, of course, and even though there may not be any reaction their souls will have been touched by this meeting of spirit with spirit. Your own heart within will expand as this recognition of God within all people and beings becomes a habit; a good habit which brings you closer to the Great Spirit within.

You will feel as though you are being carried through life like a spectator watching your life unfurl before you, meeting and overcoming the challenges and problems that occur from time to time. You will be a witness to yourself living your life each day, and a feeling of floating through life will be a treasure for you. This, then, is the aim of your life; to live out its purpose with love in your heart at all times, regardless of upsets or setups which may happen at any time.

The peace, love, joy and happiness that come to you when you live in this way will make you stand out among your fellow men and women as you live, by example, the life intended for you on the earth at this time.

Live by the Teachings

Live by the teachings and you will be following your inner soul's directions as you go through life. You all know, through what is known as your conscience, when you are living according to your life's Divine plan. You can either be carried along with the crowd or listen to your conscience, your real self, and let it show you the way. The way is different for all people, being unique to each one. Therefore, take time to link into your soul and, when the time comes for decisions, you will know from within which road to take.

Your lives are full of decision making, from personal likes or dislikes to life-changing ones regarding career opportunities, moving house, relationships or changing course on your spiritual pathway. Over the years one absorbs spiritual teachings from various sources, according to one's upbringing, conditioning or from directions within. When you feel in agreement with and accept these teachings, then you try to live your life according to them. If the teachings do not resonate within you then follow your inner promptings and your search can lead you to new philosophies and spiritual awareness of a different nature.

Whatever the outcome, and once you are at one with them, your soul or conscience will provide opportunities to live accordingly, whether it is a new way of life or continuing in your current one.

You will know from within which path to take and, when you follow the one for you, you will experience deep peace within, a deep peace that engulfs your whole being. It will enable you to meet the challenges in life that are created as a result of your decisions.

You will find that love from within will guide you as you come to terms with your new way of life and, by following the teachings that you accepted, you will love yourself, your real self, and your whole being. You will reflect that love toward all life, all people and beings with whom you come into contact. It will give you a satisfaction beyond understanding in your life as peace, love and joy shine forth in your face and demeanour wherever you go.

You will still face daily problems and normal decisions that have to be made in this life, but you will feel an inner strength and resolve that will assist you as you glide through your day in a cheerful and optimistic manner, knowing that you are on the right pathway in this glorious life.

How is your Boat?

Are you like a boat on the high seas being tossed all over the place, or are you like a boat in peaceful waters?

You all know the answer to this question. You have periods where the body seems to be thrown from pillar to post and then followed by a quiet period. Life is full of ups and downs but your real self, at the heart centre, is always still and at peace. Some people allow themselves to be continually on the move and unsettled whereas others have found equilibrium in life. The peaceful state of life can be found within and what is felt there will gradually show outwardly.

Therefore, my friends take time to find the peace within for this is the One Spirit within all life. Honour the One Spirit, revere the One Spirit, and as you make more time for meditation and contemplation on God so you will come close to All That Is. Peace and love can be seen by sensitives emitting from the heart centre when one is in this peaceful state. Once felt you will subconsciously be aware of the love within at any time in your life and you will only need to think of it, or go within, to immediately return to that heavenly state.

Your boat will appear stable on a peaceful sea, making progress as you continue life's journey in a new frame of mind, where you will become strong and resilient with the love that is emanating from you. Find the peace within, stay with it and your lives will be transformed so that people will look to you for help during the difficult times when their boat is unstable.

Once you are aware of the Great Spirit within, your life will take on new meaning with confidence, purpose and will to succeed, leading to happiness as you come to serve your fellow man on life's beautiful journey. You will be inspired from within and, as you follow your light, you will become a beacon yourself and give strength, hope and love to those you meet on the way.

Pause for a Moment

It is the time of day when all is quiet and it is appropriate to think of and feel the universal store within, the Great White Spirit, whose energy and life force is so evident and is at the very heart of all life.

Pause for a moment and rest in the beauty of this time. Feel the love, energy and peace filling every part of your bodies, and you will experience lightness and healing that can be recognised when you are in need of sustenance during the day.

The more you are in this peaceful state the more you will receive, the more you will feel, and the closer you will come to the centre of your being, the One Universal Mind.

Face to Face with the Lord

As we come to you today we appear as our real selves without any frills or baggage. This is the way to come face to face with the Great Spirit, open-minded and free of distractions, free from petty worries and unnecessary critical thoughts. When you lay yourself bare in front of the Lord you meet as you really are, ready and willing to do His will. That is not to say, of course, that you can't come to the Lord when in difficulty for that is also advised when you need help. However, we are talking about your times of meditation and your desire to be close to All That Is.

When you have preconceived ideas, and a mind full of ever-changing thoughts, then how do you expect to get close to the One Mind? It is in thanksgiving and letting your earthly attachments go, in a state of release, that you can become at One with your God or higher self. Rest a while in this bliss, this deep peace in pure silence, in the unconditional love of the Father-Mother God.

In this feeling of surrender to All That Is you will be carried along for the rest of your day and can link in at any time when you need real sustenance. This sustenance will provide you with motivation, and love for all mankind and all life. In this state you will meet all challenges with a knowing and strength that enables you to overcome your problems with ease and, at the same time, show a love for all with whom you come into contact. You will hold your heads up high as you participate fully and deeply in the day's activities, whether at work or play. An inner feeling of goodwill will accompany you at all times. It is only when you allow negative thoughts into your being that doubts and worries appear.

So, consciously seek this joyous feeling when you are in the presence of the Great Spirit. You will surmount all difficulties by your demeanour and love for all beings as you have a positive effect on your fellow man.

Remember, then, to come to the Lord in gratitude, surrender and love and a positive, glowing outlook will shine from you like a beacon at all times.

The Moment

The *moment* can last forever and it is in the moment that God created all life on earth and in the universe. The moment, my friends, is crucial to all life for everything arises and happens in the moment.

Your physical bodies were born in the moment and, as each day commences for you it starts in the moment; so, value the moment and treasure it, as your lives revolve around and have their experiences in it. Once you are in the moment it will last as long as you are unaware of any other thoughts.

Live in the moment and you are living with your God. Stay in that moment and you are experiencing Him. Continue to stay there and you will feel the love, the silence and deep peace. Time in that moment does not exist as it is like a new world with unknown treasures, where you can become lost in the wonder of the vista before you. It is only when the mind returns that time also returns to normal, as you know it.

The more you can experience the moment the more love and peace will follow you into your day, together with the knowledge and strength that will be needed, as you fulfil the promise and expectation contained within the blueprint for your life.

Journey Within

Welcome to the journey within, the journey that can transcend all others when you become at one with your real self. People talk about going within, meditating, and most have difficulty in quietening the mind. This is because, normally, the mind is busy sifting through all the many thoughts that are popping in and out all the time.

So, it takes practice to calm the mind and allow your real self to appear, to come to the forefront. It is always there, of course, but it takes time to appreciate this and still the mind and thus become One with God. When you do achieve this the rest of your body and mind become still and a feeling of peace may engulf you. Stay in this state and soak up the love and healing that is generated from there, your real self, which is the Great Spirit within all life.

There is no need for words at this time as overwhelming love takes over and, by giving your lower self to All That Is in this way, the body is healed and rejuvenated with the light from within. You have surrendered yourself to your God in such a way that it feels natural and very alive to be part of the universal Spirit as the lower self is left behind and the higher self takes over.

Your life will then become a living example of all that is good in mankind. The light of the Father within will shine before you as you take yourself onto the stage of life in such a confident and loving manner that you will have a positive effect on your surroundings and the people who come in contact with you.

Inner Light

As you go within, in the silence of the day, you come close to your real self, the self that is light and by which we can recognise you. This light varies in intensity according to your openness and desire for union with the Great Spirit. Take time to sit and rest in the beauty: let the light envelop your whole body and you will feel encased in love.

So, stay a while like this and you will find that peace, that deep peace within, which will enable you to meet any problems or challenges that occur in your lives. Know that the spirit is within you at all times and not just when you are meditating. You can link into your soul at any time, and by doing so throughout your day you will be on the chosen pathway for you. As decisions need to be made you will know the right road to take.

Stay aware and alive to your inner reality and you will be receptive to receive the inspiration that will assist you to help others on their own personal pathways.

Feel the love of the Father all around you as nature springs back into life; know that God's love is ever-pulsating through all life and, as you become aware of the Great Spirit within all life, you become at One with Him.

One-Pointedness

One-pointedness toward the Lord thy God can mean directing all one's attention to the God within; you may call it devotion or at Oneness but one-pointedness describes exactly the way to commune with the Great Spirit.

Some people have difficulty in being still, even for a moment, and find it even more difficult to be silent, silent in the mind, away from the turmoil of endless thoughts. Others make time to be quiet and on their own, for to commune within you can find the very centre of your being, where there is silence like no other, peace so deep, and love that envelops you and makes your whole vision within expand before you.

The more you are able to come to the Great Spirit in this way the more you will experience Godliness, the silence when you can hear a pin drop and peace that is so deep that it encircles you. It fills your body and your surroundings and the love permeates through you in such a way that your fingers tingle and enables you to reach the point where you are no longer aware of yourself, as your attention has been drawn into the centre of the beautiful Oneness. All thoughts and feelings can be left aside as you dwell in the Lord's space.

You are then experiencing the I AM within you. This state can last for one second, or a lifetime, but usually until the mind comes in and spoils it all. However, once you have been in this inexplicable and glorious state you can return at any time provided that you have the one-pointedness and determination to lose your outer self and dwell with the Lord.

Communion with Spirit Within

We come to you today with love and peace in our hearts as you come close to the Great Spirit. It is not easy to continually be in that space which appears blank but is, in fact, the embryo for all life.

As you let yourselves go deeper you will find a beauty within, an indescribable peace which leads to an apparent expansion of the heart area. It is filled with love and warmth of the spirit and becomes a rich glow. As the body is filled with light, in this state you receive the bliss of the Father within. This bliss is the natural state of spirit within you.

Most people have lost the ability to be in this wonderful state as they are usually chasing after material desires. However, when one makes time to be in communion with the Great Spirit then your life takes on a natural rhythm, which draws to it all that is needed to live a life dedicated to the Father. A clear pathway emerges where all needs are met and you are inspired to follow your life's unique plan. You will find people and situations appear before you as you live out your life of service to mankind.

The love you send out, whether consciously or not, has a far-reaching effect and people are drawn to you as they pick up the light and magnetism surrounding you. So, stay in this beautiful bliss throughout your day, not in meditation, of course, but once your day has started in this manner the light from within automatically fills your whole being and goes before you as you complete the tasks of your day.

Your lives will never be the same once you have touched *reality* in such a way that it reverberates in and around you, so that you feel lasting peace and love within you at all times. Many people before have experienced this beautiful communication with the Great Spirit and have endeavoured to describe it for others. This is not easy as each of you will experience it uniquely as to befit you.

So, my friends, go in peace and love with renewed confidence and bearing that will enable you to achieve ambitions long ago discarded before you come to, and appreciate, the love of your Father within.

At One with All That Is

As you find yourself within you are peeling away the layers of material thoughts that may keep you from your reality. Continue then to come to that great centre of your being where the Almighty Spirit resides.

Feel yourselves become closer and closer as you leave behind those thoughts. You are now in a ball of light, of pure white light. It surrounds you and *is* you, and as you linger there you will find that perfect peace and silence. It is from there that you will feel at One with all life and, as you stay in this moment, something remarkable happens to your body. It becomes filled with the light and love of the Father. You will feel yourselves expanding to the far reaches of the universe.

You are now at One with All That Is. You feel at the centre of everything and while you stay in this glorious moment you are at the centre of all life. Therefore, take this love, light and peace into your day and it will go before you as you enter again your material world. Know as you do this what strength and beauty is within you.

You can retain this experience within as you become embroiled in your day-to-day activities. Be aware at all times of the love and light of the Father that is within you, and it will be reflected in all you do and in the way you relate to everyone you meet in life.

Retain the confidence, the love, the light and the truth that is within you and, if necessary, return to that glorious spot within as you continue to fulfil life's journey that is unique to each one of you.

Conscious, Conscience, Consciousness

Conscious, conscience and consciousness: three similar-sounding words with three different meanings. You are said to be conscious in your normal human state. Your conscience is like your soul, which speaks to you with what is called the still small voice. If you listen, your conscience lets you know when you are deviating from your chosen pathway.

Consciousness is similar, but not the same as it is the all-encompassing Spirit. The consciousness is the whole of which you are all part and integrated. When you are in meditation, having shut out your normal thoughts and feelings, you are close to your real self and part of the total consciousness. It may sound a big word, and it does have a big meaning: it is the intermediary state of the Great Spirit for humans to feel part of God, and is like a large stepping-stone to the pure Spirit of the Godhead.

So, when you feel you are becoming centred within your consciousness is still expanding. Consciousness gives you knowledge and wisdom through different avenues, either direct, in meditation, through channels, books, or by word of mouth. As you grow you will feel part of the general consciousness of the earth, its people and all life.

As you go deeper within, your consciousness will expand further. When you reach the centre of your being you will feel that you are in the centre of the Great Spirit and you will realise that you are at One with all life.

You will be at the centre of the universe, the centre of the material and spiritual life and completely at One with the Father-Mother God.

Enlightenment

As you sit in meditation and come close to your real self, the spirit, the outer mind will close and leave you with the vision within. This does not happen immediately for, like all things worth having, they have to be worked at and practiced.

You do have clues or little experiences on the way because when the mind temporarily closes down the soul takes over with the result that you may sense a whole new world within. When the time is right you will feel the peace, love and light within and it comes with a state of Oneness.

Rest a while in this beautiful gift of the Father-Mother God and, having left behind all the concerns and day-to-day thinking of the outside world, you are able to explore the glories of life within. You don't have to do anything; you will just be in the presence of the Lord. Beautiful colours will abound and, as the feeling of peace becomes deeper, an unbelievable bliss will flood your whole self.

Your vision from within feels wider, filling the whole world and the universe as you experience, with the Great Spirit, the core or nucleus of all life. This, my friends, is enlightenment.

Once you have touched it you will want to stay there forever. This, of course, is not practical in your life on earth, but once having touched that special state within you can return to it at any time.

Your experience of enlightenment, even though only for short periods, will enable you to go through life with a knowing that the One Spirit is within you and all life. This will give you real security, confidence, well-being and a feeling of love and peace at your very centre, which will enable you to sail through life with happiness untold to handle all life's various experiences.

The light that goes with you will attract souls in need of spiritual help and sustenance and you will feel completely fulfilled as you enter the wisdom and teaching period of your lives.

I AM in You and You are in Me

'I AM in you and you are in Me'. You have heard this before but does it really resonate with you? When you sit back and analyse these words they can only mean that when God created the world and the universe He created *all* life. He created mankind as an extension of Himself so that His Spirit is within mankind, and all life on the earth and throughout the universe.

My friends, we are all spirit: the only difference between us is that you have physical, tangible bodies as a means of experiencing life on earth. We, on the other hand, have ethereal bodies that we can use and adapt, as necessary, during our life in spirit. When you become one with your spirit, the One Great Mind, you too will feel that you have an ethereal body when you are in meditation, or are still and in the silence. It is only when you move around and start using your mind that your physical bodies come into use again.

However, when you are in the glorious state of Oneness all things are possible. You can affect the future and the past as you are transformed into spiritual awareness enabling you to go anywhere from within. This, of course, affects your bodies and life on earth, so when you are continually in touch with your real self a whole vista of life's opportunities is laid before you.

Some of you may be worried about the responsibility of the new-found freedom that would have been created for you. It is nothing to fear and it could not be further from the truth. Your new relationship with the One Spirit will enable you to go through life without worrying over decisions. Your life will be so exquisite it will feel like you are almost running on automatic and decisions will already have been taken as you carry out the love in action that you were born to do.

Part Six

Into the Future with Awareness and Love

Welcome

Welcome to this inner space from where your love, the love of the Father, originates. In the deepest crevice of your heart is the nucleus of the Divine I AM. Meditate on the I AM within you, feel the light and healing go through your whole body, and watch it go forth as beautiful white light surrounds everyone within its path. Like attracts like and as it permeates life there will be an opportunity for people to find their own light within.

There has been so much written about enlightenment that it often frightens people and creates a barrier. Enlightenment is simply recognising the I AM within you and within all life; feeling at One in the now, where time stands still and one feels surrounded by unconditional love. You see the light and feel deep peace.

So, you can all experience enlightenment briefly, regularly, or permanently. Some people have a sudden enlightenment which will then stay in the background and can again be experienced whenever the mind relaxes into it. Others feel enlightenment when in meditation and touch on it only briefly but, once they have experienced it, even only briefly, then their whole being is eager to have the experience again.

There is no mystique with it and it can be felt whenever you let go of all material and outer thoughts and sink into that glorious light and love. Experience, then, this Oneness of all life and let yourself return to the bliss of eternity where you will receive inspiration and direction in your life as you are aware of the One Great Spirit within.

Change

We join you in your meditation in the quiet hours of the morning when all is apparently asleep and when you can feel the silence. It is as though every physical move pierces the silence, the silence of the Great Spirit where all is contained and within Whom everything is created, or renewed, as nature awakens from its slumber.

So, are you all ready to awaken from your slumber, the slumber of ignorance, lack of knowledge and awareness of who you really are and what is behind your lives on earth?

Yes, you have had your religions over many centuries, you have prayed to your God, however you imagined Him to be, but very few have really understood the truth, the wisdom of the ages. That is why it has been necessary in every era to send teachers to earth to remind you of the eternal truths. Unfortunately, for the majority, they have shunned this great news as they thought they knew better. While there have always been relatively few who understood the real truth the rest were not open or ready to receive it.

Times are changing, my friends; people have had enough of the old ways as their lives are not as they would have expected. Why is this, you may ask, for there have been so many technical advances in the last century that you have, so to speak, all the tools necessary to live successful lives, but people have forgotten who they really are. The time has come for them to look within themselves to find the answers to the time-honoured questions of 'Who am I?' and, 'Why am I here?' While there is some literature available on the subject most people are too involved in their own lives and problems to ask the questions, let alone be ready and alert to receive the answers.

The time is fast approaching when this situation is about to alter as the changing vibrations continue to increase gradually on your earth. Until now very few have felt the change, and even they have only felt it marginally. However, for those who have and are embracing this new spiritual atmosphere on earth it will be a wonderful experience as you feel the warmth and glow of the unconditional love of the Great Spirit as it opens up from within a glorious new phase of life for you.

You will help create the foundation for radical spiritual understanding for all people, as you spend time with your Father within, and you will be given all the knowledge and help needed to take your world into the next chapter of the Divine plan, where unconditional love will be flooded all over the earth. For those who have and are being prepared they will use the conditions to help mankind to usher in the new Golden Age of love and goodwill to all people.

So, look out for subtle changes within yourselves and your planet, and as you get closer to the Great Spirit so you will be fulfilling His Divine plan for you.

In the Now

Yesterday is gone, tomorrow is not here, so all there really is, is this moment, the now. Rest in this moment from which everything emanates and is created, for it is in the now that the Great Spirit just is.

Where do you think revelations, great pieces of art and unique inventions come from? It is in the moment or now, within, when it is like being in a different world where all is still, silent and that deep, deep peace abounds.

Therefore, make your life a series of moments as it is not usually practical to sit in meditation all day in the moment. So, whenever possible just pause and be in that glorious, fulfilling and wondrous now.

You don't have to take yourself away from the crowd; you can just feel that moment within wherever you are. Whether it is for one second or a million seconds you will be at one with your real self, which is your God within.

Peace Within

All is quiet. All is as it should be. Feel the deep peace, the deep peace within. Notice how you come to your heart centre when you look within. For although the Great Spirit is within every cell of the body and, indeed, all life, the heart centre is the very point in the body where the Great Spirit can be felt.

As you recognise the Great Spirit within feel the warmth, the love, expand in your body as it reaches the very tips of your fingers and the extremities of your head and feet. Don't let the love and peace stay there let it go out to all people in need and to the four corners of the earth.

As you consciously feel this love-energy go forth notice the joy within that goes with it. The more you send out the more you receive, for God has a limitless supply of love. Sit in peace, enjoying the moment where you are acting as a transformer. God's love comes into you and is transformed into the energy necessary in the world today, both for its people and the planet itself.

As you open yourself, your inner self, for this purpose you will feel peace, joy and bliss within. Stay like this as long as you can and know that you are helping with the Divine plan for the earth at this time.

Sunrise

What a pleasure it is on your earth when everything is awakening to the morning sun. People used to be awake and outside to welcome in the new day at sunrise. Some still do, especially at equinoxes, but the majority of people are fixed in their ways and habits, preparing for work or other activities. There was something special about welcoming the sun as it reinforced for one the Greatness of the Almighty, the Creator of all life.

Being present at sunrise also has an effect on an inner level, as it feels that one is welcoming in the great force. It is, of course, already there within all life but people tend to forget this as they are absorbed in their own worldly affairs. Take time, therefore, even if you don't attend sunrise, to make a point of feeling the Lord within.

As you devote time to experience the love and peace within, you will not only experience a flood of energy across your body but you will also be aware of it all around you and, as your day progresses, so you take this unseen love-energy with you. It is always there my friends; you only need to spend a little time in being aware of it within. Not only will your day be transformed, but so will others as they feel the light and love when you come near to them. They will then also have the opportunity to feel the love for themselves.

As love goes around the earth it appears to come back to you and the cycle begins again. Love cannot stand still, it envelops everything within its path. People will, therefore, have the opportunity to participate in and be aware of this great truth.

Meditation

At the start of each day it is good to sit in meditation, endeavouring to clear the mind to allow the real self to take centre stage. As you do this you will feel a warmth in your heart centre, which may be followed by seeing images, the beauty of a lotus flower or rose, for example.

Stay in the moment and the whole body becomes enveloped in love and a slight tingling sensation could take place. As you become more engrossed in the moment outside worries and concerns disappear. The longer you stay in this moment the deeper the silence. Stay there and you will be close to the very centre of your being where the Great Spirit of all life is located.

As you go ever deeper words and thoughts recede, leaving you in that glorious heavenly state of Oneness.

Silence in the Moment

It is a different world within, my friends, a world of silence, inner silence. There may be noise all around in the outside world but it is silent within. You could say it is a golden silence, for many see gold amid an array of colours when they are meditating and coming close to their real self.

The silence in the moment can lead to deepest peace. Nothing matters in this moment as thoughts are far away as you feel your heart centre expand in love. This is all happening within the moment, the now. Rest in this peace and love, when the body is forgotten, and the feeling within takes over as you are left with a vista leading to infinity, containing indescribable quietness and beauty. You are now in a state of consciousness which is close to Godliness. You will then feel engulfed by, and become at One with, the Almighty Great Spirit.

In this non-duality state all differences disappear as there is only the One. Your problems and daily activities are forgotten and yet, when you return to your normal conscious state, your inner strength has become stronger with unconditional love still oozing from each cell of your body. Your large problems now become little difficulties easily dealt with by your newly gained confidence.

You can return at any time to that incredible place within, which will renew your enthusiasm and joy for this wonderful life on earth.

Meditation in Love and Service

In the early hours of the morning, when all is still, the silence is accentuated and a whole new world opens up within. My friends, stay in this moment as long as you can, for peace and love will permeate your whole being and even the air and the room you are in. This love and peace, although not seen, will be felt by those who come in contact with you.

This love, originating from the Father, is so strong that it travels far and wide. Those of you who sit and meditate in love and service to mankind achieve results far greater than you can possibly realise. It gathers pace and comes together with the love throughout the planet and is used to subdue so many of the negative thoughts surrounding the earth at this time. So, never have any doubt that your actions are not worthwhile as they help collectively, not only the planet and its people, but also you yourselves.

The time is coming, as the increased vibrations begin to take effect, when people generally will need help to explain their new feelings, uncertainty, and a wish to let go of the old restrictive thoughts and ideas. There will be a strong notion for people to seek out explanations of how they feel. Those who have indicated their willingness to be part of the new spiritual order on earth will come forward in groups, formed for this purpose, throughout the world. They will show people, by teachings and example, that a lasting peace will arrive as the teachings and love of the Great Spirit become prominent in all walks of life.

Go forward then, my friends, with heads held high, giving out the joy to be felt by all as the new Golden Age starts to be seen and experienced by each and every one of you.

Holy Grail

Why do people search for the Holy Grail as though it was a glittering object out there, when everyone's real Holy Grail is within? So many people and so much time is spent searching outside when they only have to look inside themselves to find the fountain of all knowledge. The great Masters taught this truth for so long and yet the number of people today following this truth is so small that it is less than one per cent of the population.

This is really quite extraordinary when we have all the different religions and spiritual organisations teaching that love is within. Many people may appear to look within, but most give up before they find the glorious truth for themselves. Many others are apparently too busy to make time to look within and the great majority either lack this knowledge or are just not interested.

So, to those who have found the beauty, the glory of the Spirit within, although being in a minority, they have found the jewel in their lives. This enables them to come to that special place at any time, but especially when they feel a need to be close to their God. Once this has been fully experienced one's life is transformed and the special feeling within can be with them for the rest of their lives. It will give them enjoyment and fulfilment with a desire to help mankind in service of one form or another.

The day is coming when more and more people will follow this great teaching and become at one with their real selves. They will come together in love and peace and others will join them in the name of love. There will be no need to have names or titles for organisations as this movement will be instigated and inspired by God through the people.

As the numbers increase manifold a new era will dawn on this beautiful earth and a period of joy and happiness will accompany the start of the new Golden Age that has been predicted for so long.

New Dawn

We come together again in love and peace with our hearts wide open to receive God's love, and with our arms wide open to be channels for the love and healing needed to herald in the new era of heaven on earth.

As you empty yourselves of material and everyday thoughts and worries so you become harbingers for the New Age. You, who are willing and able to be of service to mankind, have prepared yourselves for this time. Be always in touch with your inner selves, in that place beyond description, and you will be ready with a knowing to carry out the message and plan of the Almighty.

Be, therefore, in that God-space, my friends, ready for any eventuality and, as you come together with like-minded people, so you will be given the confidence, the words and, above all, the love and peace of the Great One.

A new dawn has come and you will be part of the change, ready and willing to play your part in this exciting and auspicious time in the history of this wonderful God-made earth.

Primordial Love

We come to you today to speak of love, that small word with such a huge meaning. The word love conjures up different meanings for different people. The primordial word love means that energy from the One Great Intelligence, who created the earth and the universe and all life as you know it. This love is tangible and can be felt within. It is within each atom, each cell of your bodies and when you are able to link into the love of the Father you will feel a surge of energy throughout your being.

This energy, which is responsible for maintaining all natural laws and rhythms of existence, is never ceasing. It is abundant and continually replenishing itself and you can be aware of this great love by going within to the centre of your being where the Lord resides. His love can be felt there and, as it expands within, it is pulsating and waiting to be sent forth to the rest of mankind, the earth and all life.

As you feel this love going out it is being replaced manifold and the warm glow you feel within will expand to the extremities of your bodies. As you stay in this beautiful state nothing can disturb your relationship with your Maker within. Take this God-given love, energy and strength with you through your day and be ready at any time to tap into it. That wondrous love within will inspire you and take you beyond the limits you have set yourselves in this life.

So, be in touch at all times and you will experience the treasures given to you as you explore new journeys and paths in life with the Great Spirit within.

The New Heaven on Earth

We come to you today with a glorious message that all is as it should be, as the Divine plan is in place for the new heaven on earth.

This is happening with the higher vibrations that are gradually being brought to the earth. Slowly at first, and like a snowball gathering momentum and more snow as it becomes larger, the increase in vibrations will gradually be felt across the board as lightness in people's minds and bodies. If you feel a slight loss of balance for brief moments, which are not normal, then this is confirmation that the action is taking place.

Be assured that this is only for the good of the earth and mankind for the changes will affect the subtle body of the earth and people and, in time, will also have a positive effect on the physical bodies. Those of you who are sensitive may already feel this lightness in and around you. There is nothing to be afraid of, as an overwhelming feeling of well-being will occur gradually across the planet.

The Golden Age, which has been forecast and, indeed, talked about for many years will actually come into the hearts and minds of the people. Some of you will start to feel warmth and welcoming signs within and in time will come forward through the many groups that are being formed throughout the world. They will assist in the explanation and spiritual teachings that will be needed by the population to commence a transformation in their inner selves, resulting in a change in their way of life within the new limitless condition of the human mind.

You are all entering into this prestigious time in the history of the earth as the foundations will be set for all to welcome in the most wonderful Golden Age for mankind.

Epilogue

We look at your world and see a dense cloud, unlike your weather clouds, that surrounds the earth at this time. It has built up over many centuries from man's inhumanity to man in thought, word and deed. Most people cannot see this cloud. Although it became thicker in the last century there are now areas throughout the world where love has pierced this cloud and left holes in it. This has occurred where more and more people, like yourselves, meet together and send out their love to all in need.

As these holes enlarge the cloud will eventually disperse, leaving mankind with the start of the new Golden Age. There is much work to do before that is achieved, my friends, for this cloud covers more than 95% of the earth. We look forward to seeing an expansion of these groups and, with it, the beginning and extension of the break-up of this cloud.

Your people, in the main, are and have been for some time going through a period of ignorance of the spirit. Stand up then, my friends, as harbingers to lead the way in showing the world that love without arms conquers everything and everyone.

Be ready then to take up your arms of love and, with God at your side and within, you will succeed in this important project.

Joyful One

Appendices

The following pages are included to record some of my experiences over the last eighteen months. These complement and give additional clarity to the main message of the book and some are also included in this section which do not readily fit into the main body of the text.

Appendix A Personal Letters

Making a selection of personal letters between Joan and I has been both a pleasure and a difficult task. There were approximately one hundred letters which have been whittled down to nine. It is hoped that these will give an idea of my feelings when receiving and sending these communications. As previously explained I was very surprised to channel the letters as I certainly had no intention to write to Joan, nor any expectation of a reply. Some parts are very personal but they were a tremendous comfort to me. Apart from my initial incredulity they also gave useful information regarding passing to the next world.

20 June 2012

Darling Joan

I have known you for many lifetimes. This latest life has given me a sense of unconditional love.

That feeling between us was, and is, so special and makes us inseparable.

You were so patient and full of understanding when I was learning how to look after you and myself. The way you taught me to cook was a fine example of not giving up on me when I was learning. I should have learnt a long time ago but you didn't complain, just helped when I was ready.

Well, my precious is this the way we are going to communicate, or can we manage to do so by thought? We shall see!

I love you with all my heart and soul; take care and know I am always here for you in some form or other.

Rich

*

29 June 2012

My precious

I love you. You mean the world to me. I love your personality, your generous ways and I shall always remember the times you cared for me, you made me feel so special and helped me through my ordeal.

I love you greatly and even more than before, if that is possible. The things I feel for you are magnified over here, as are all thoughts and experiences, including re-living our experiences together on earth.

I love you. I do hear you all the time when you speak to me and I was pleased to help you in the garage recently. Yes, your upstanding light went a day or so ago, glad you fixed it. Must look after your eyes, I was helping you to buy the other reading light, isn't it good?

We will never be parted. So-called death cannot part love. Remember me always as your best friend, lover and partner in life there and here.

Well, I can't tell you what is in store for you but know that we shall be together and there is nothing to fear. Your healing will get stronger and you will be used more and more, but there are other things planned which you will love.

All my love always.

Joan

27 September 2012

Dearest Rich

Well, where do I begin? I was with you on Tuesday when you 'let it all out', going over our last few weeks together on the earth plane. It was emotional for me, too, both at the time and on Tuesday. Your memory in that respect is excellent. What a journey for you, for us both.

Yes, I did know within that things were getting worse. You were tremendous, how you dealt with the situations, starting with the CT scan when Louise came with us. She was great, even though she didn't know what was happening. You, poor thing, having to deal with all the ambulances twice. Don't know how you coped, especially at the end with contacting the boys.

I will forever remember your caring and the efficient way you dealt with everything. It was not easy, despite me trying to make it that way. Things change over time and all went perfectly.

I must let you go to rest your back, it's not been good for a while but it will get better soon and you can resume your life of giving and playing; wonderful.

I love you unconditionally.

Joan

3 November 2012

My precious Joan

I love you so, so much that I could yell it over the rooftops. Thank you for all your help with the words for the cards.

We all had a good day today and I know you were with us; good new place wasn't it? I am sure you were with me last night for the healing. It was good. You certainly get around with Sue even if you had not met her here. You seem to be very good in these situations as I am sure you are in connection with the articles I receive. What about the latest ones and the progression to the A4 paper?

I still find it all quite incredible really and wonder what is going to happen next. I shall just have to continue with pen and paper at the ready. You know why I am not quite 100% sure of it all yet, because we used to talk about communication from your side and how things can be misinterpreted. Please let me know if possible if all this is hunky-dory and that my imagination has not gone wild. I feel it is right in my bones, but a little confirmation would not go adrift.

I often look at your photos my darling and can't really believe that I shall not see your physical presence again. I love you so much and would love to hold you in my arms like I used to.

However, what is happening, the communication, is marvellous and the next best thing. You said you would try to communicate and you have certainly made a tremendous job of it.

Thank you. I love you.

Rich

10 November 2012

My darling Rich

I love you my precious more than all the stars in the universe. I haven't spoken to you like this for a few days and I have missed it very much. You are receiving words regularly and you are always quite taken aback when you read them again.

It is incredible and you are becoming a good channel and we are all looking forward to the next stage. Keep being aware and ready, it is great that you started meditation again, after all that time without for both of us. It is a little different for me now and we, especially I, appreciate what you are doing, especially your willingness to help.

Jan has been asking if I have any comments to make now I am here. Yes I do, in fact I wish to say that we see things from a different perspective, but our beliefs are much the same, except that they are deeper and with a keener insight.

However things are not black and white as, for instance, in terms of reincarnation. In as much as all life continues then that is correct but the method by which a soul part or segment, or group member returns can vary. This depends upon many things, such as progression, past experiences and future requirements in that progression. It is very difficult to explain and indeed quite complicated. I would go so far as to say even with the knowledge I have, some people with a similar amount still do not believe in it.

Of course one of the prime reasons is to gain more experience and, if this is not required, reincarnation may no longer be appropriate, unless there is a different reason for it, such as teaching or following the Divine plan. You see I could go on and on about it, but I will leave it there for now.

All my love, always.

Joan

My darling Joan

Do you remember when we walked between the tall redwood trees; we felt the peace and purity of the air. I have so many wonderful memories of our time together, a treasure where we felt at one in the later years. We spent the earlier years getting to know each other so well, our experiences before the children, then bringing them up, and the later years after they left the nest. I know we all had some hard times but, overall, they were magnificent years and I am so grateful that we had each other for so long, as my love for you grew into something really special. I will never forget those times and certain experiences keep coming back, especially after seeing some old photographs.

Now, I feel you here with me although I miss your physical presence so much. What I do remember is our excitement at having met, becoming engaged, getting married, having children and the marvel of our support for one another. I feel you supporting me now, as I sit alone, and as I enter this new phase of spiritual growth. I am hanging in there for that one as the writings get more frequent and explicit. I am sure you are here when I am writing but, as you appreciate, I keep trying to empty my mind to let the words come through untainted. What a test, as you had often called me 'monkey mind' partly in jest.

Weren't we so blessed to go to the feet of Sai Baba and be in his presence for such a long time? We didn't think of those days as work, it was just the right thing to do.

Oh, such memories! I love you deeply and trust you are happy and fulfilled where you are.

Rich

23 November 2012

Hello my darling Rich

I love you my precious more than you will ever know. I am with you when you feel lonely and I also remember our wonderful times together.

You have been my rock for so many years. I may have had ideas and organised things but I could always rely on you to keep at it, especially when the going got tough. You were always there in the good and bad times and I, too, have such great memories.

My darling I am pleased that the writings are getting stronger and more detailed and everyone here is delighted. It is true about getting enough good sleep. You always were able to switch off and fall asleep. You needed to then and you will need to now. This is funny me telling you this when I am keeping you up. I am sure you will soon be asleep anyway. I will soothe your brow and help you sleep, you will see.

My darling those years together are a treasure to me also as you described in your letter. We were made for each other and when we had differences we always made up and it was enjoyable.

You are wondering where all this writing is leading and you know it is developing well. You will soon know more and you are right, I am involved but not as the main scribe. He is the monk that you were told is your guide. He is such a gentle soul with such knowledge and is so wise. We were all together in previous lives.

Yes, I am learning a little of the past but only as much as I need to know. You referred to my life here and I can confirm it is very rewarding and fulfilling. As you would expect I have met most of the friends and relations who were here before me. All are doing well and say hello to you with many blessings and much love.

I see your beautiful soul and work with you when you are asleep, also preparing for this work. You seem more relaxed about it now and things will be good, you will enjoy the work.

Joan

*

12 February 2013

My darling Rich

I love you so very much. I know this is a difficult time for you and I am with you. I am around you and in you, I am you and by your side always. You can't help thinking about our time together and I do too.

Obviously it was very difficult for you but peaceful for me and I was aware that I was ready to transcend the divide into the next life. It was so peaceful with a brilliant light and a wonderful feeling and I saw my Mum and Dad and Duncan. I got used to the wonderful feeling here and what we talked about, being as one in our lives. I was the one who said that we were not individual and that helped me on arrival. You coped very well as I knew you would and we both missed each other.

Things have worked out so well with the channelling. I promised to come back to you my love and I think you will agree I have been successful. I sit with you now in your meditation as you 'come to' in the mornings.

I love you more and more each day; we are so far yet so close my darling. Take time, don't rush, and don't feel you have to do anything at the moment. Be in that wondrous Divine love we all have the opportunity to experience and I will be there with you.

I love you.

Joan

13 February 2013

My darling Joan

I love you my precious more than I can describe. Our life together was quite amazing and we were made for each other. Our spiritual growth together was a Divine gift and I shall always be grateful that we had, and I assume still have, similar beliefs or knowing.

You are now involved in translating these teachings into words to be transcribed for others to see or hear. What an incredible outcome of our life together and your short time on the other side.

I love you so much and felt you so close tonight sharing the letters we both received through our inner beings in the early communicating days. They are quite remarkable and I am so grateful for this ongoing treat.

May we ever be so close in spirit and continue on the planned pathway in the future. I love you and look forward to our next communication.

Rich

Appendix B Circle Meetings

The articles and prayers given by Joyful One to my friends and I at our regular circle meetings will give an insight into our experiences and, at the same time, provide further teachings for the perusal of the reader. The teachings cover various topics including the Akashic Records and the coming of the Golden Age. We were also privileged to receive a talk by a visitor from the higher realms. It was noticeable that the teachings came in such a friendly, respectful, courteous and loving manner, making it a real pleasure and resulting in our eagerness for the next meeting.

23 April 2013

The scene has been set; you are all receptive on this beautiful morning in your world. We come to talk today about the beauty in your hearts, the beauty of the Great Spirit, whose manifestations can be seen everywhere. From the brightest blue sky to the blackest cloud He is present, so by feeling and knowing His presence within you are coming to the centre of all things. The centre of all life is *within* you my friends.

We know this is very hard for people to accept, especially those who do not see beyond their noses, and it is even difficult for those who have some understanding. How can the centre of the universe be within each one of you? Simply, my friends, because the Lord is within each one of you and, wherever His presence is felt, or seen, or known, that is the centre of His totality for He is omnipresent, as some of you have experienced. So, if you consider the Great Spirit is in all life, and you are part of that, then how can this revelation be brought forth across the lands?

It will, my friends, but as you would imagine it couldn't happen immediately for, if the Almighty lifted His hand and changed everything immediately, where do you think that would get us? Wonderful for a short time but gradually things would return back to how they were. So, the Divine takes his or her time to work through slowly so that more and more come to the ancient truths.

As we speak there are identical groups, such as yours, receiving similar teachings and, before long, the world will come to know that something great and unusual will be taking place. They will need explanations and this is where people like you will come in.

We have heard it said 'We have heard all this before, many, many years ago. You keep promising that the Golden Age will appear.' Well, we are saying to you that it has already started, my friends. The higher vibrations are here, and will be increasing, so believe, my friends, and you will see things starting to change in your lifetimes and we will rejoice with you as you start to see this happen.

I would like to finish this first part on a joyful note and leave you with your hearts and souls in tune with one another and with us.

14 May 2013

Yes, my friends, we are still here and come with joy to listen with you to a visitor from the higher realms who has been attracted to this abode.

> I AM the way, the life.
> I AM your life, I AM all life; I AM.
> I AM the smallest beetle, the largest elephant.
> I AM the earth, the universe, All That Is; I AM.
> I AM the song of the bird, the cry of the elephant, the roar of the lion, the music of the piano or the violin, the oboe and the drum.
> I AM the song and the singer, I AM the poet.
> I AM the words, the poetry and the prose; I AM.
> I AM with you all at all times; you need only take one step to me and I will take one hundred to you.
> Open your hearts and minds to Me and I will be there as I always am, waiting to hear from you.

I AM ready to inspire you, to give you inventions, the words for
songs and My teachings.

When you are open to receive I AM there.

I have always been and I always will be; as you will be also.

Remember Me at all times and you will feel My presence so
strongly that you will feel that you are being carried through
life by Me.

Be ready to receive My word for I AM always ready to help you.

Take time to contemplate on these words and feel My love
permeate throughout your bodies and beyond.

I AM ready, are you?'

28 May 2013

You are surrounded, my friends, by angels and we have invited some
dear souls who are in need of these conditions. We welcome them
and ask them to open up to these conditions. Let them take in all they
need and reflect on it in time to come. For the rest of us, and indeed
all of us, we have a special visitor who would like to address you.

'We bring the blessings of the Creator today as you soak up these
heavenly conditions. We would like to speak to you of the need to
revolutionize the teachings and spiritual thoughts, beliefs and actions
of your people on earth. It is God's will that a change is due and you
are aware of subtle changes already taking place. The raising of the
vibrations of the earth, its atmosphere and all its inhabitants will be felt
by all, but it is already being felt by those who are sensitive.

'Although you may feel that the effects are not always pleasant
these will pass and you will feel yourselves raised internally. You
will then have a boost of energy and light to enable you, and people
like you, to take the next step. We have already said that there are
groups throughout your world and they are being given the same
information. Be a little patient and carry on as you are and before long
you will be given more information and be brought together with
other like-minded people.

'We are aware and can see that you are being prepared and are willing to undertake whatever is necessary. We thank you for this and will help to bring the conditions within you to establish the right footing from which this work can take off.

'We have enjoyed spending this time with you and thank you for your attention. As we leave we spread our blessings over all of you.'

04 June 2013

We join you as ever in happiness and joy and look forward to spending a delightful time with you this morning. You are all ready and we have been joined as usual by others who wish to experience time in this beautiful atmosphere.

We welcome you all and would ask you to feel the actual silence, for it contains everything. It is the embryo for life; where there is silence there is the Great Spirit. The Great Spirit manifests in you all, whether seen or unseen. So, from this silence pure energy arises, the energy of love which controls all life. It is the foundation and the experience of life. Without it no life would exist, there would be no people, no universe. Can you imagine the earth without its people, animals, birds and vegetation? No, it is unthinkable and the Great Spirit has every intention to continue this beautiful life on earth.

Many people take their lives for granted and before they realise it they are middle-aged and wonder where the time went. Others have too much time on their hands and they think life is just one long bore. How can there be so much difference with the busy person who has no time and at the other extreme where there is too much time? As in most things the middle road is the most beneficial, where you have time to think and meditate about life and appreciate God's gifts to you all. You can take in the fresh air, feel the dew in the morning, smell the roses and appreciate all life at all times.

When you come to the understanding that all life is God then, within you, you have this background sense of joy. Even though you may be busy you are aware of it within you. Take more time, if you can, to experience this joy in everything you do. Even if the people you meet are not aware or do not experience the joy within, you know it is there, nevertheless, and will only need a spark to set it on fire.

We feel the joy within you and know it will last forever, as it will with us. Remember as you go through life to spread joy and happiness wherever you go. As we are sure you have found out it is returned to you manifold.

We leave you to meditate on this joy which can be felt by all of us.

25 June 2013

My friends, we wish to tell you a little this morning about the Akashic Records. Some people have heard of them, others pooh-pooh them but we can assure you that they exist and have done since the start of time. They are obviously not like files on earth because you would have run out of space many a long age ago. They are more akin to the ever-decreasing size of files on your computers but even they wouldn't be sufficient for the complete records... No, they are entirely different but they do record every single life and every action and thought within that life.

There are ways that you could see parts of the records but normally they are not open to people on earth. They are very helpful once people traverse to this side of life but, even then, there is a restriction on how much an individual may receive from his previous lives. It does not just refer to individual lives, my friends; it also contains the history of the earth and of the heavens. It is enormous in your worldly terms and does contain the history of how life started in the physical and heavenly spheres. We cannot go too deeply into these records but when necessary, to be of service in one way or another, we are given the assistance to obtain whatever is required for selected purposes.

You would be amazed to see within them and we have been privileged to see certain sections. So, remember, everything that happens is recorded. This is not in any way a threat, it is just information, as we don't wish to judge. On your side of life, for example, you only see one side of an argument whereas we see far more but not the whole situation. Therefore, none of you or us should judge.

There is an interaction and, as the beautiful light which surrounds all of you increases or decreases according to experiences, this interacts with the Akashic Records and so assists in the beauty that is presented by your souls to us on this side of life.

We hope we have given you a little insight today and, as you go further along the spiritual road, so we will be pleased to pass on more treasures that are hidden until the key and door is ready to be opened for you.

02 April 2013

O Great One, who is in the forests, in the sea, in the centre of the earth and the sun and all life.

We come to You with love in our hearts and ask that Your knowledge, truth and wisdom be shared with us today, as we sit expectantly in peace, ready to absorb Your love into our whole beings, that we may offer ourselves in Thy service.

Amen

28 May 2013

O eternal One Spirit of all life, we revere You and come to you in awe of Your wonders and greatness.

You are not seen and yet You are in the heart of all beings. Without You, Great Spirit, there would be no life, no earth and no universe.

We see before us the manifestation of Your nature, where there is order within the trees, flowers, insects and the animal species, together with birds and the fish in the sea.

We thank You, Great Spirit, not only for this life but also for providing everything we need.

We pay homage as we come closer to You each day on our pathway back to You.

We, of ourselves, are nothing. May we therefore remember at all times who we really are.

Amen

Appendix C Personal Teachings

Further extracts from personal teachings by Joyful One are included here. These offer advice concerning the purpose of the circle and help relating to this book. As you will see it is the teaching aspects of some of the communications that are shown. These include attitudes, friendship, discoveries and inventions, age-old wisdom and man's spiritual quest. There is also information on the process of channelling.

05 December 2012

Friendship and love is the key to a happy life. Why do some people seem to make friends easily while others have very few? For those who don't, could it be that they are sending out the wrong signals that do not create any attraction?

It is all about one's attitude and expansive thoughts that bring friendly contacts. Love, my friends, is behind everything. To open oneself and give love to one another is the greatest way to live. Love of your God and love of God within all life is the key to happiness. You don't have to like and get on with everyone to love them. It is that recognition of the God within all people and beings that automatically leads to loving them.

So, we say to people who can't seem to make or hold on to friends, seek the love within yourself and then love yourself for who you really are, regardless of what you have done in the past. You are sons and daughters of the Great Spirit. It, therefore, follows that once you love yourself you will love all people and beings that come into your orbit. You will find that your circle of friends will expand and the love you give out will bring its own rewards.

When this love for one's fellow man and woman expands into all aspects of life, i.e. in the workplace, in politics, in local and national government and recreation, it will grow into one great family within a country and, eventually, internationally. This is what is needed at the current time so continue to send out light and live a life of service to mankind.

05 January 2013

Cardiac arrest occurs when the heart stops or beats uncontrollably fast. Many years ago this would have resulted in death but, as the medical profession have made advances in both the knowledge and equipment to treat this condition, nowadays patients usually recover.

Where or how do doctors learn new skills in dealing with accidents and medical conditions? They have ideas put in their minds, during sleep or other suitable times, from this side of life. When people pass to the next life they do not lose their skills so when they again become used to life here they usually want to serve humanity in some form or other.

As we have been talking about doctors we will continue using them as an example, to show the way people can follow their urge to serve those on earth. We have the equivalent of your schools and universities with our own laboratories, etc. and we have made great advances in the way to treat medical diseases and accidents on earth. Complete healings and recoveries from various incidents cannot be released to earth all in one go so they are gradually introduced by the methods already stated. However, it must appear to those on earth that these are their ideas and inventions and can cover a multitude of services, commercial and industrial prototypes. Also, in the art and fashion worlds discoveries appear to be made all the time on earth. In fact, in any category you may like to mention, you will find that this is happening as the earth and its people continue to evolve.

The amount of information to be passed has to be carefully balanced to ensure that certain new ideas do not happen too quickly and, although they are always done with the best intentions here, we cannot govern your free will and your decisions on how to handle the new information. You can imagine the responsibility for the decisions here are taken seriously and at a high level. We also have to take into account the general conditions, both natural and man-made, and as we can see a little way into the future this is also in the equation.

There are many other services undertaken to help mankind, including what are known as guardian angels, guides and helpers in healing, clairvoyance, teaching and other guidance. All this help is available but can only be used for people on earth with their permission, which may be direct or on a soul level. There are many methods adopted by us that include light, sound, vibrations, magnetism, rays and other scientific systems not yet known to mankind.

We have to be aware of natural laws, such as cause and effect, Divine plans and the overall effect of our various work. In addition we must also take into account the condition of the earth itself and the way that nature, people and national governments are acting and reacting as this is continually subject to change. So, take this knowledge, meditate on it, and you will be directed from within to follow your soul's pathway in this life.

20 February 2013

You bring with you into this life a certain level of understanding which you may not be aware of at first, but your heart recognises certain aspects of it and also rejects certain ones, like many of today's philosophies.

We wish to take you back to those times when people thought the world was flat. This was way before inventions when man lived closer to nature and, as such, cared about his environment, family, friends and immediate surroundings. They communicated with the nature spirits, which helped them understand how to grow and obtain food without upsetting the natural flow of the weather and seasons. They worshipped the sun and the moon and thanked God for the rain and the sunshine. Life was simple then yet people, as now, were inquisitive as to who they really were. They watched nature in all its glory and knew that there was some Great Spirit behind and within all life.

So, we move on to today and, in spite of all modern inventions, transport, and the work of scientists, people still raise the inevitable question of who they really are and where they come from. Countless teachers over the centuries have explained the Fall of Man when the devil notion was first introduced. The devil, my friends, does not exist other than in one's own, if you like, lower self when the mind has doubts and dark thoughts. Why would God create something like a devil to undo all His work? It is a figment of man's imagination and reflects one's fighting within oneself rather than any outside spirit. That is not to say there are no demonic influences or devil-like souls in existence.

However, God is pure Spirit and can never be touched by negative thoughts. You came to the earth to experience a wide range of thought forms from pure to very clouded and, although you do not have the memory, you certainly have the influences and feelings of previous experiences. Therefore, one's latest sojourn is for the development of the soul and maybe to experience life as a tramp or, alternatively, as a high-flying businessman. You will all, over time, have experienced the riches and rags of life on earth, but you return with a sackload of experiences, feelings, love, hate, desires and, as they are bundled up, you realise how much you have learnt both through adversity and pleasure.

We, on this side of life, look at your religions and are both intrigued and dismayed by what has happened to the original teachings of the founders. All your religions preach the love of your fellow man and yet, without fail, they have a history of rising up against one another, thinking one is better than the other. Many thinking people on earth today are looking for deeper understanding, but that is not to say that organised religions do not serve a purpose. Of course, there are people with love in their hearts who live wonderful lives preaching the various gospels. However, there is a greater movement today of people wanting to explore their own spiritual feelings within and they are looking at ancient wisdom, untainted by the strictness and narrowness of the creeds and laws of today's religions.

Many people go all over the world to places of spiritual energy but really all have within them the knowledge and wisdom to find the answers to life's problems. From time to time throughout history teachers have been sent to the earth and while large numbers

213

recognised the love and spiritual greatness of these Masters, the people sometimes turned on them through envy or jealousy. So, return to yourself, your real self within and find your own truth, your own pathway and values.

Feel within the wonders of the universe so that you become transformed from a child of God to a spokesperson for all that is true and beautiful in this world of yours. Know that you will receive all wisdom, strength and power to undertake the very purpose of your incarnation.

23 March 2013

We come close to you as you meet us with a willingness to move forward in your quest for knowledge, wisdom and truth. You have opened your real self to us so that we can communicate as though we were in the same room as you on a physical level. We are in the same room but on a spiritual level and, as we make this communication, the feeling of love is so evident for the pooling of resources, so to speak, it enables this transmission to take place.

You have wondered how it works, my friend, and, in fact, are still wondering. We do, indeed, put thoughts into your mind but unless you are open, with a desire to be of service, then these thoughts would just disappear as thousands of thoughts in the day come into your mind and then disappear. So, you have prepared yourself, with our help, making yourself available by opening up to us and concentrating on the channel within you to receive these thoughts.

Your make-up is such that we use your brain to convert these thoughts into words. It is not easy to perform and achieve the desired results. To you it feels like being in that centre of love within you and, as such, you are able to keep at bay all those other thoughts that would normally be around you at this time. We utilise your vocabulary and certain understandings in order to convey the message that we wish to get across. Without your love and ours this would be impossible.

It is remarkable from your point of view and, indeed, it would feel that way to us if we were in your shoes. However, we can see and know a little more from where we are and it seems quite natural to us, but we do appreciate your time and devotion in providing this channel for us.

Appendix D Quotations

The quotations from Eileen Caddy's *Opening Doors Within* have been included to show an uncanny resemblance to the overall message of the book. The extract from the introduction to *The Aquarian Gospel of Jesus the Christ* gives the strong message that man has always been and always will be. This extract was particularly important to Joan. Also included are two short quotations, favourites of Joan, one by Rabindranath Tagore and the other by Ralph Waldo Emerson, the latter describing one of her attributes. Finally, an inspired article written by Joan, several years ago, is included as a tribute to her character and beliefs. She, it was, who started this communication process with her friends on the other side with utmost sincerity and love for the Almighty Great Spirit of all life.

Eileen Caddy's *Opening Doors Within* - 29th May

You are the point of light within My mind. You are the point of love within My heart. When you can accept it, when you can see yourself as the microcosm of the macrocosm, you will never again belittle yourself or think ill of yourself. You will realise that you are indeed made in My image and likeness, that we are one, and that nothing and no one can separate us. If you feel any separation from Me, it is of your own making, for I never separate Myself from you. You are individually what I AM universally. Is it any wonder you have to be born again to accept the wonder of this truth? So many souls have strayed so far from Me, and have separated themselves to such an extent that they have placed Me in the heavens at such heights that I AM unapproachable. I AM within you, hidden in the very depths waiting to be recognised and drawn forth.

Eileen Caddy's *Opening Doors Within* - 17th July

See that everything you do is dedicated to Me and is of benefit to the whole. When you live for the whole, the self is forgotten in service to your fellow human beings, and when you are serving them, you are serving Me. All is so closely intertwined that you cannot separate one from the other, I in you and you in Me. I AM in everything and everyone; therefore I AM in your neighbour, in your friend and in your enemy alike. Wherever I AM, there is love, for I AM love. Fill your heart and mind with love, for everything and everyone responds to love, as love draws the very best out of all. Where love is, there My Spirit is, and where My Spirit is, there is the source of your spiritual life. Seek always that which is deep within you, and waste no more time seeking for the answer to life from without.

Eileen Caddy's *Opening Doors Within* - 19th July

Do not just talk about the new heaven and new earth; it is up to you to bring it down into your life to make it reality. Do not talk about love and loving; live it so that all can see what it means. Words without action are meaningless and useless. They are like hot air that evaporates into nothingness. You are to bring down My kingdom on earth by the way you live and behave, so your life is an example, a joyous example, which all will want to follow. No one wants to go through life over-burdened, lacking joy and spontaneity. Blessed is that person who brings joy to those souls who are burdened and lack sparkle in life. Cast all your burdens upon Me, and bring joy and freedom to all those souls you contact. Be joy and inspiration, and reflect Me in all that you do, say and think. Be at perfect peace as you do My will and walk in My ways, glorifying Me.

'Time never was when man was not. If life at any time began a time would come when it would end.

The thoughts of God cannot be circumscribed. No finite man can comprehend things infinite.

All finite things are subject under change. All finite things will cease to be, because there was a time when they were not.

The bodies and the soul of men are finite things, and they will change, yea, from the finite point of view the time will come when they will be no more.

But man himself is not the body, nor the soul; he is a spirit and is part of God.

Creative Fiat gave to man, to spirit man, a soul that he might function on the plane of soul; gave him a body of the flesh, that he might function on the plane of things made manifest.'

Death is not extinguishing the light.
It is only putting out the lamp because dawn has come.
Rabindranath Tagore

Some pursue happiness, others create it.
Ralph Waldo Emerson

Wanting Less and Giving More by Joan Brake

To want less is to loosen all desires that keep us glued to the imperfect being of *ego*. For to desire that which is an illusion of our reality is foolishness, indeed folly. For in all things there is nothing to substantiate the craving of desire. To desire is to acknowledge ignorance of being, for in truth all things are already ours if we did but practice our Divinity. Seeing all as One, not separate, is to be that which we desire so there is no need for desire: all is ours always. Truth is the backbone of understanding that all things exist for the love of God. In understanding this, the need or desire for anything subsides into peace.

What do we need to do, therefore, to give more and want less? We need to recognise the Divinity that holds everything together, that is love. Sai Baba said 'love is the foundation of all things, it is the engine of being, the cause of creation, the millstone of ego.'

When love fills our being there is a flowing of giving, giving, giving, then all we want to do is give because of the fullness of giving. To desire love is to desire God in fullness. When we feel and experience the fullness of love, all other desires and wants fade. When it is experienced, a new strength appears which manifests in humility through a knowing of the vastness and power of love.

Sai Baba said "This morning shadow moves in front of you, however fast you run you cannot catch it, on plain or mountain. Or the shadow may pursue you, and you cannot escape from it. This is the nature of desire. You may pursue it, or it may pursue you, but you cannot overcome it or catch it. Desire is an insubstantial shadow. But turn your desire inward toward spiritual treasure, then it yields substantial results."

Love is not a romantic toy to play with in our spare time: it is that which we seek constantly in our lives, and yet it is our very being covered with conditioning. We follow the pack by wanting more and giving less, instead of following the One by giving more and wanting less.

Lightning Source UK Ltd.
Milton Keynes UK
UKOW03f0723190914

238791UK00003B/78/P